image comics presents

THE WALKING DEAD™

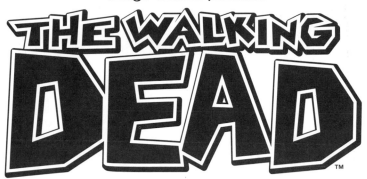

ROBERT KIRKMAN
CREATOR, WRITER, LETTERER

CHARLIE ADLARD
PENCILER, INKER

CLIFF RATHBURN
GRAY TONES

TONY MOORE
COVER

for image comics:

Erik Larsen
Publisher

Todd McFarlane
President

Marc Silvestri
CEO

Jim Valentino
Vice-President

Eric Stephenson
Executive Director

Brett Evans
Production Manager

Allen Hui
Production Artist

Mia MacHatton
Administrative Assistant

Missie Miranda
Controller

B. Clay Moore
PR & Marketing Coordinator

Joe Keatinge
Traffic Manager

Jonathan Chan
Production Assistant

THE WALKING DEAD, VOL. 3: SAFETY BEHIND BARS, April 2005. First Printing. Published by Image Comics, Inc., Office of publication 1942 University Avenue, Suite 305, Berkeley, California 94704. Copyright © 2005 Robert Kirkman. All rights reserved. Originally published in single magazine format as THE WALKING DEAD #13-18. THE WALKING DEAD™ (including all prominent characters featured in thi issue), its logo and all character likenesses are trademarks of Robert Kirkman, unless otherwise noted. Image Comics® is a trademark o Image Comics, Inc. All rights reserved. No part of this publication may be reproduced or transmitted, in any form or by any means (excep for for short excerpts for review purposes) without the express written permission of Image Comics, Inc. All names, characters, events an locales in this publication are entirely fictional. Any resemblance to actual persons (living and/or dead), events or places, without satiric inten is coincidental. PRINTED IN CANADA

www.imagecomics.com

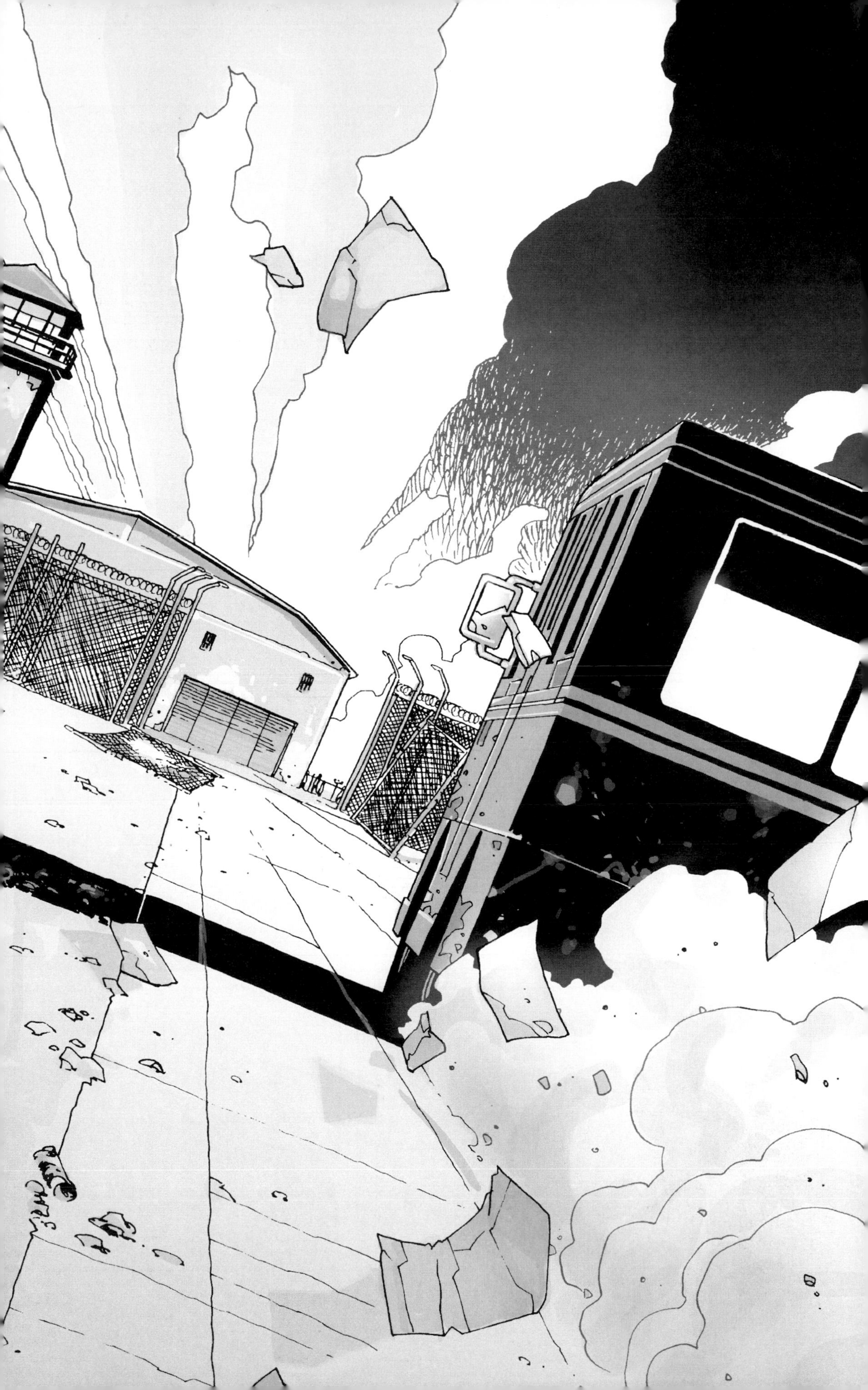

PLEASE TELL ME THAT'S THE *LAST* TIME WE'RE ALL GOING TO HAVE TO PACK INTO *THAT* THING.

I DON'T KNOW...

...THIS PLACE NEEDS A *LOT* OF CLEANING UP.

OH, MAN... I DON'T HAVE THE *ENERGY* FOR THIS.

DON'T TELL ME *THAT,* TYREESE. IT'S LOOKING LIKE I'M REALLY GOING TO *NEED* YOU IN A COUPLE MINUTES.

IN *FACT,* IF WE DON'T THINK OF SOMETHING *SOON,* WE'RE GOING TO HAVE TO FILE BACK INTO THE RV *RIGHT NOW.*

OH, HELL.

GUYS--I THINK WE CAN PULL THIS *GATE* CLOSED. COME GIVE ME A *HAND.*

WOW--FEELS A LOT DIFFERENT ON *THIS* SIDE OF THE FENCE.

DON'T FORGET HOW MUCH *FASTER* WE ARE THAN THESE GUYS. JUST DON'T LET YOURSELF GET SURROUNDED.

IF YOU HAVE TO RUN--*RUN*.

OKAY... LET'S *DO* THIS, PEOPLE.

TYREESE AND I WILL DO THE *DIRTY* WORK. YOU HANG BACK AND IF WE LOOK LIKE WE'VE GOT *TOO MANY* OF THEM COMING AT US AT ONE TIME, PICK THEM *OFF*.

I WANT TO KEEP THE SHOTS FIRED TO A *MINIMUM*. I DON'T WANT TO CAUSE THEM TO SWARM US.

THIS IS GOING TO *SUCK*.

JUST *LOOK* AT THIS PLACE, IT'LL BE *WORTH* IT.

THUKK!

IT *BETTER* BE.

THWAK!

SHUKK!

SPLAK!

HUNGH!

WROK!

SPAK!

BLAM!

BLAM!

SKRAGG!

WELL--I THINK THAT'S *ALL* OF THEM.

YOU THINK? IT SEEMED LIKE THERE WERE SO MUCH *MORE.*

I DON'T KNOW--WE KILLED A *LOT* OF THEM.

THANKS FOR THE *SAVE* BACK THERE, BY THE WAY.

TOLD YOU I'D BE USEFUL.

HAARRRNNNHHUNNGGHHH!

YOU GUYS HEAR THAT?

WHAT *IS* THAT?

I THINK IT'S COMING FROM INSIDE.

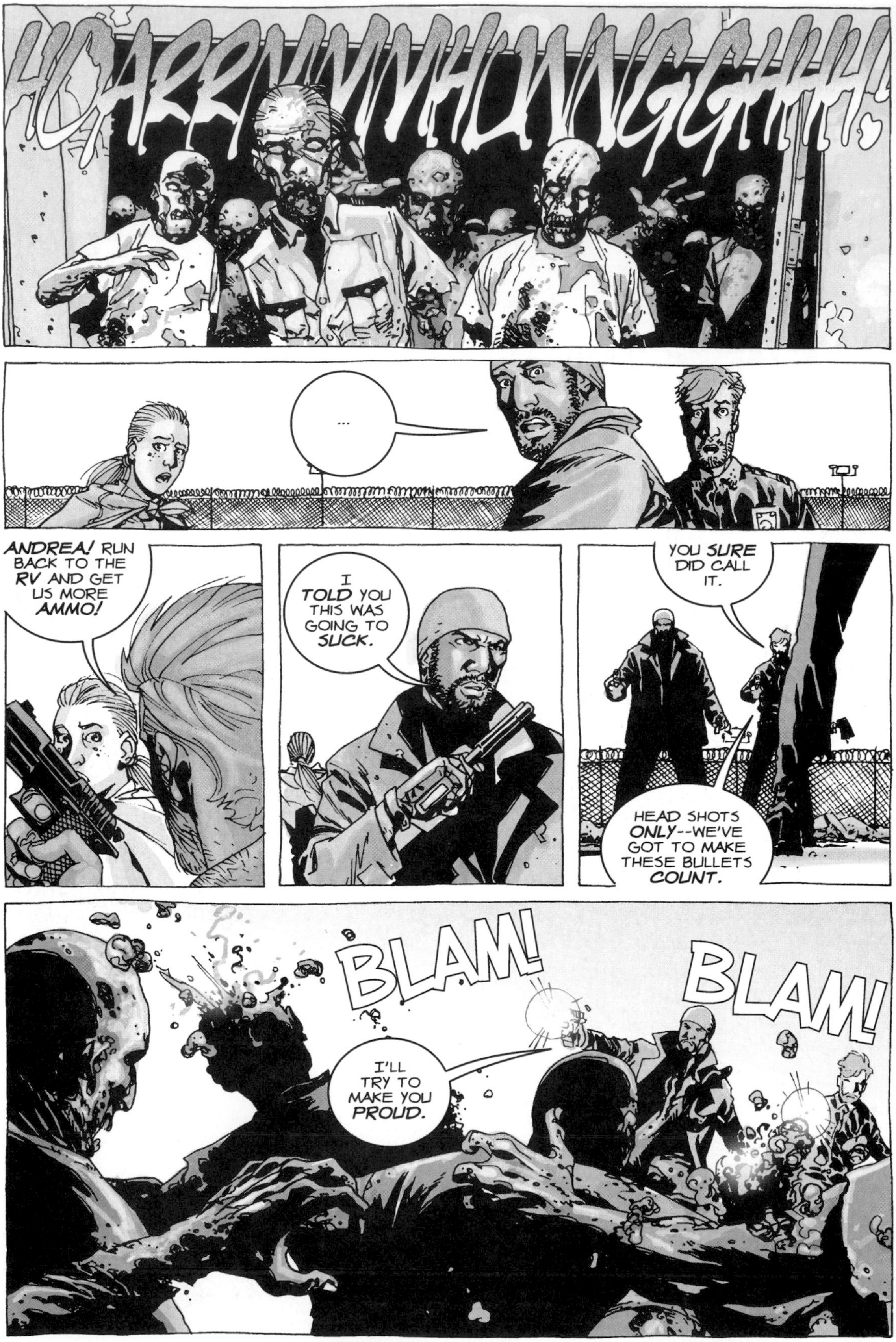
HOARRMMMHUNNGGHHH!
...
ANDREA! RUN BACK TO THE RV AND GET US MORE AMMO!
I TOLD YOU THIS WAS GOING TO SUCK.
YOU SURE DID CALL IT.
HEAD SHOTS ONLY--WE'VE GOT TO MAKE THESE BULLETS COUNT.
BLAM!
BLAM!
I'LL TRY TO MAKE YOU PROUD.

BLAM!

BLAM!

THUKK!

BLAM!

I DON'T LIKE THIS, MAN. THERE'S *WAY* TOO MANY OF THEM.

IT AIN'T *THAT* BAD. WE CAN *ALWAYS* RUN AWAY. JUST STAY CALM...

...AND PRAY ANDREA COMES BACK WITH MORE BULLETS SOON.

BLAM!

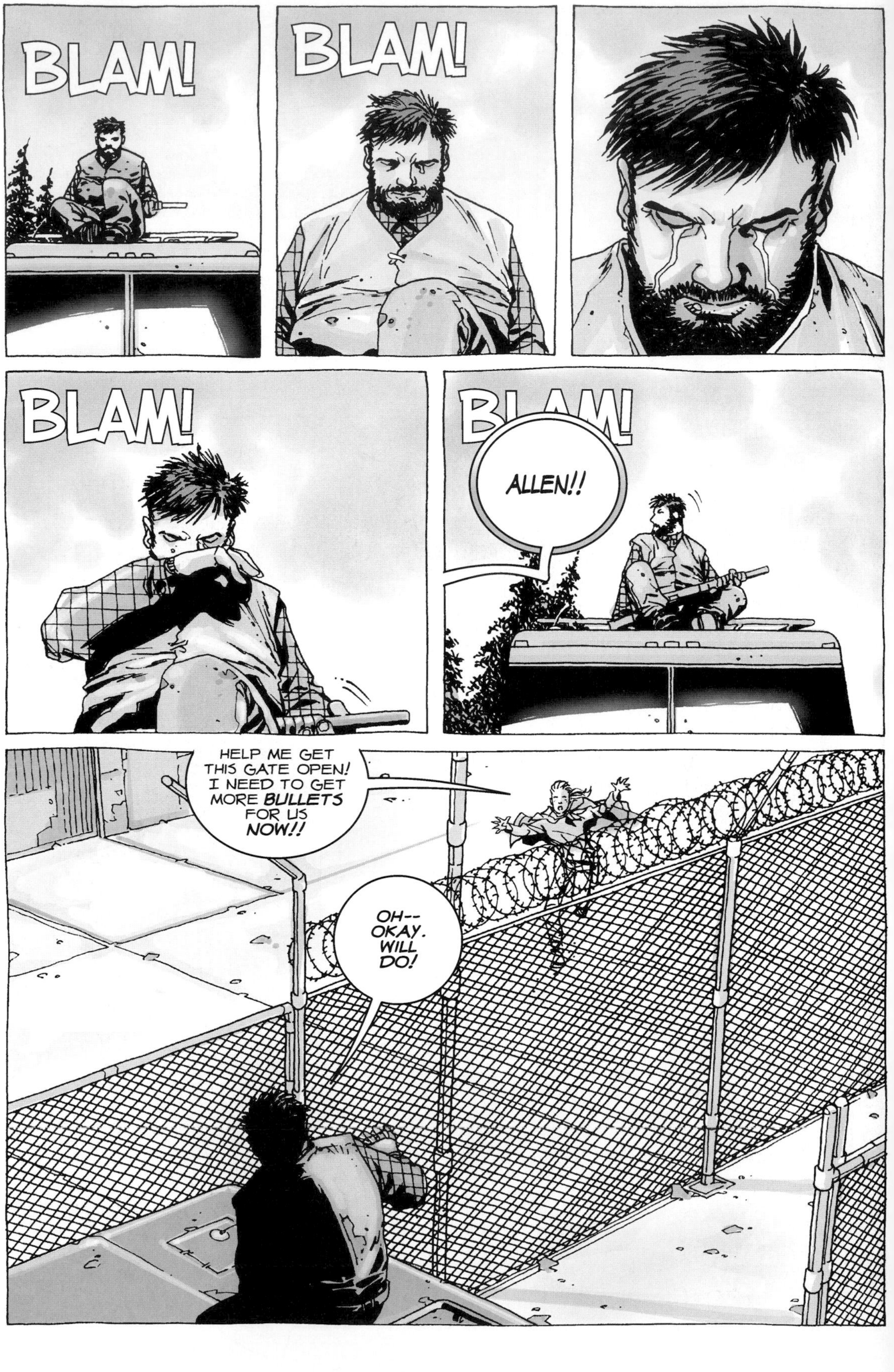
BLAM!
BLAM!
BLAM!
BLAM!
ALLEN!!
HELP ME GET THIS GATE OPEN! I NEED TO GET MORE BULLETS FOR US NOW!!
OH-- OKAY. WILL DO!

THIS IS *FUCKING BULLSHIT*. I'M ALMOST *SEVENTEEN*. I'VE GOT A GUN, I DO OKAY AT TARGET PRACTICE. I SHOULD BE OUT WITH RICK AND TYREESE SHOOTING *ZOMBIES*.

NOT IN HERE, FUCKING *BABYSITTING*.

YOU SHOULDN'T *CUSS* SO MUCH. I KNOW YOU'RE *NOT* AN ALL THE WAY *ADULT*. SAYING THOSE SWEARS ISN'T GOING TO *FOOL* ME.

SHUT UP, *BRAT!*

CHRIS, *STOP IT!*

C'MON, *SOPHIA*... LET'S GO UP FRONT AND PLAY *GO FISH*. I THINK *ALLEN* LEFT HIS *CARDS* OUT.

CALL ME A BRAT...

HOW MANY DO YOU *NEED?*

AS *MUCH* AS I CAN *CARRY!*

HOW *BAD* IS IT?

PRETTY *BAD.*

THESE ARE *ALL* THE CLIPS THAT ARE *LOADED*--AND A TON OF *LOOSE* BULLETS. IF YOU GUYS MOW THROUGH THESE CLIPS YOU'LL HAVE TO LOAD UP *NEW* ONES IN A *HURRY.*

I'LL LEAVE THAT HONOR TO *TYREESE.* HE'S ALMOST *USELESS* WITH ANYTHING OTHER THAN THAT *HAMMER* OF HIS.

THANKS!

WHAT WERE THEY *TALKING* ABOUT?

I DON'T *KNOW.* I SHOULD HAVE TOLD THEM THAT *CHRIS* WAS BEING *MEAN.*

YOU READY TO *PLAY?*

UH-HUH. YOU GO *FIRST.*

DO YOU HAVE A *BEARDED* GUY WITH A BLACK UPSIDE-DOWN *HEART?*

...AND DO YOU WANT TO BE MY *BOYFRIEND?*

NO WAY! *GROSS!* YOU'RE *DISGUSTING!*

GO *FISH.*

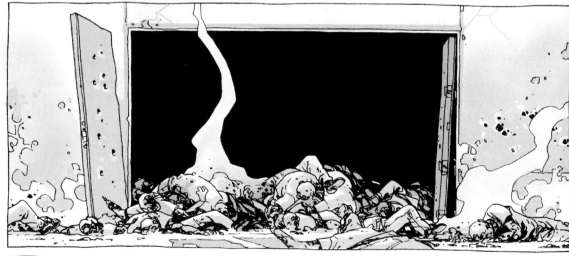

WE'LL BURN THE REST *TOMORROW.* THEY'RE NOT IN OUR WAY AND I JUST DIDN'T HAVE THE *ENERGY* TO GET THEM FAR ENOUGH AWAY FROM US TO BURN BEFORE DARK.

YOU SOUND LIKE YOU'RE *APOLOGIZING.* WE'RE ALL JUST AS EXHAUSTED AS *YOU* ARE, RICK--WE *KNOW* WHAT YOU'RE GOING THROUGH.

YEAH-- ALLEN'S *RIGHT.* WE NEED TO FIND SOME FOOD, *QUICK.*

I'M *HUNGRY,* MOMMY. I WANT SOME *FOOD.*

I *KNOW* HONEY--*I'M* SORRY. WE JUST DON'T *HAVE* ANY.

SORRY. I DIDN'T MEAN TO BRING IT UP.

TOMORROW WE'LL HAVE EVERYTHING WE NEED FOR A GOOD *LONG* TIME. THIS PLACE HAS *GOT* TO HAVE A *STOCKPILE* OF CANNED GOODS.

HOPEFULLY IT WAS OVERRUN BY THE *UNDEAD* BEFORE IT COULD BE *LOOTED* BY ANYONE.

YEAH, HOPEFULLY IT'S JUST FULL OF FLESH EATING *MONSTERS* AND OUR *BAKED BEANS* ARE STILL *INTACT* IN THERE.

IF SOMEONE HAD SAID LAST YEAR THAT I WOULD *EVER* UTTER THAT LINE OUT LOUD... I'D *STILL* BE LAUGHING *NOW.*

JESUS-- I'D LOVE SOME *BAKED BEANS* RIGHT NOW...

I'M **WAY TOO** PREGNANT. **TRUST** ME.

OH, **STOP IT.** YOU'RE BARELY EVEN **SHOWING.** SAVE THE **COMPLAINING** FOR WHEN YOU CAN'T **STAND UP** WITHOUT HELP.

DON'T WORRY, I'LL HAVE **PLENTY** OF **COMPLAINING** LEFT WHEN THE TIME COMES.

OKAY, **LISTEN UP,** PEOPLE!

I KNOW **EVERYONE** IS **HUNGRY,** AND ANXIOUS TO GET **INSIDE** THIS PLACE AND SEE JUST HOW LIVEABLE IT REALLY IS. I KNOW I **AM.** TYREESE AND I ARE **GOING IN.** WE'RE GOING TO SWEEP AS **LARGE** AN AREA AS WE **CAN** AND MAKE SURE IT'S **CLEAR** AND **CLOSED OFF** FROM THE **REST** OF THE PRISON SO THAT MAYBE... JUST **MAYBE** WE WON'T HAVE TO SLEEP IN THAT **DAMN** RV TONIGHT.

WHILE WE'RE IN THERE, I WANT **LORI, ANDREA,** AND **ALLEN** ON ZOMBIE BURNING DETAIL. DRAG THOSE CARCASSES OUT TO WHERE WE BURNED THE **OTHERS** LAST NIGHT AND TRY AND CLEAN OUT THE PRISON GROUNDS. IF WE'RE GOING TO **LIVE** HERE... I'D LIKE TO GET **RID** OF ALL THAT STUFF.

DALE. I WANT **YOU** TO BE AT THE GATE WITH A SHOTGUN, WATCHING THEM DRAG THE **BODIES** OUT. MAKE SURE THEY'RE IN THE CLEAR AT **ALL** TIMES. WE DON'T HAVE **MANY** SHELLS OR BULLETS **LEFT**--SO USE THEM **SPARINGLY.**

CHRIS AND JUILE... YOU'RE BABYSITTING IN THE RV **AGAIN.** I KNOW IT'S NOT VERY **EXCITING** BUT I NEED TO MAKE SURE YOU KIDS ARE SAFE. HOPEFULLY AFTER TODAY YOU WON'T **NEED** TO DO THIS ANY MORE.

I THOUGHT WE COVERED THIS *YESTERDAY*. I'M THE *BEST SHOT* HERE. I SHOULD BE *INSIDE* WITH YOU TWO.

IN AN OPEN AREA, *YEAH*, BUT NOT *INSIDE*. I'D RATHER NOT *USE* OUR GUNS UNLESS WE *HAVE* TO. IT'S AN ENCLOSED SPACE, WE COULD GET *SURROUNDED* IF WE ATTRACT THEM *TO* US.

WE *DON'T KNOW* HOW MUCH *LIGHT* WE'LL HAVE *EITHER*. DO YOU KNOW WHERE GLENN'S FLASHLIGHTS ARE? I KNOW HE LEFT THEM *WITH* US.

I THINK I KNOW *WHERE* THEY'RE AT. I'LL BE RIGHT *BACK*.

PLEASE BE CAREFUL IN THERE, *RICK*. I'M GOING TO BE WORRIED *SICK* OUT HERE.

RELAX, HON'. I'LL HAVE *TYREESE* TO PROTECT ME.

I GUESS *NOW* WOULD NOT BE THE BEST TIME TO ADMIT TO YOU THAT I'M AFRAID OF THE *DARK*.

FOUND THEM!

I'LL LET YOU HOLD *BOTH* FLASHLIGHTS IF YOU *WANT*.

C'MON. LET'S *DO* THIS.

WE'LL BE BACK SOON. BE *SAFE*.

YOU *TOO*.

YOU'RE IN *LUCK*, TYREESE. LOOKS LIKE WE WON'T BE *NEEDING* THESE FLASHLIGHTS. AT LEAST NOT IN *THIS* AREA.

MAN, *RICK*...THIS IS *NICE.* WITH ALL THESE WINDOWS... IT'S NOT *DARK* AT ALL. I WAS REALLY WORRIED THAT IF WE MOVED IN HERE WE'D NEED TORCHES OR CANDLES OR *SOMETHING.* I WASN'T LOOKING FORWARD TO LIVING IN THE *DARK* MOST OF THE TIME.

YEAH, THIS PLACE IS *GREAT*, BUT DON'T GET *TOO* COMFORTABLE. IT'S MORE THAN LIKELY STILL GOT A *FEW* OF THE *OLD* TENANTS LEFT AND JUST BECAUSE WE'LL BE ABLE TO *SEE* THEM DOESN'T MAKE THEM ANY LESS *DANGEROUS.*

I *HEAR* YOU.

HUMGH.

GAH!

TWACK!

KINDA *JUMPY* THERE, EH? YOU NOT EXPECTING TO SEE *ANY* OF THESE THINGS IN HERE?

HEH.

OH *EAT* ME. I'LL BE *MORE* WORRIED ABOUT ME WHEN THE SIGHT OF THOSE THINGS *DOESN'T* STARTLE ME.

THAT DAY HAS *COME* AND *GONE* FOR ME *LONG* AGO, MY FRIEND.

LUCKY YOU. LIGHTS ON... IT'S GETTING PRETTY *DARK* BACK HERE.

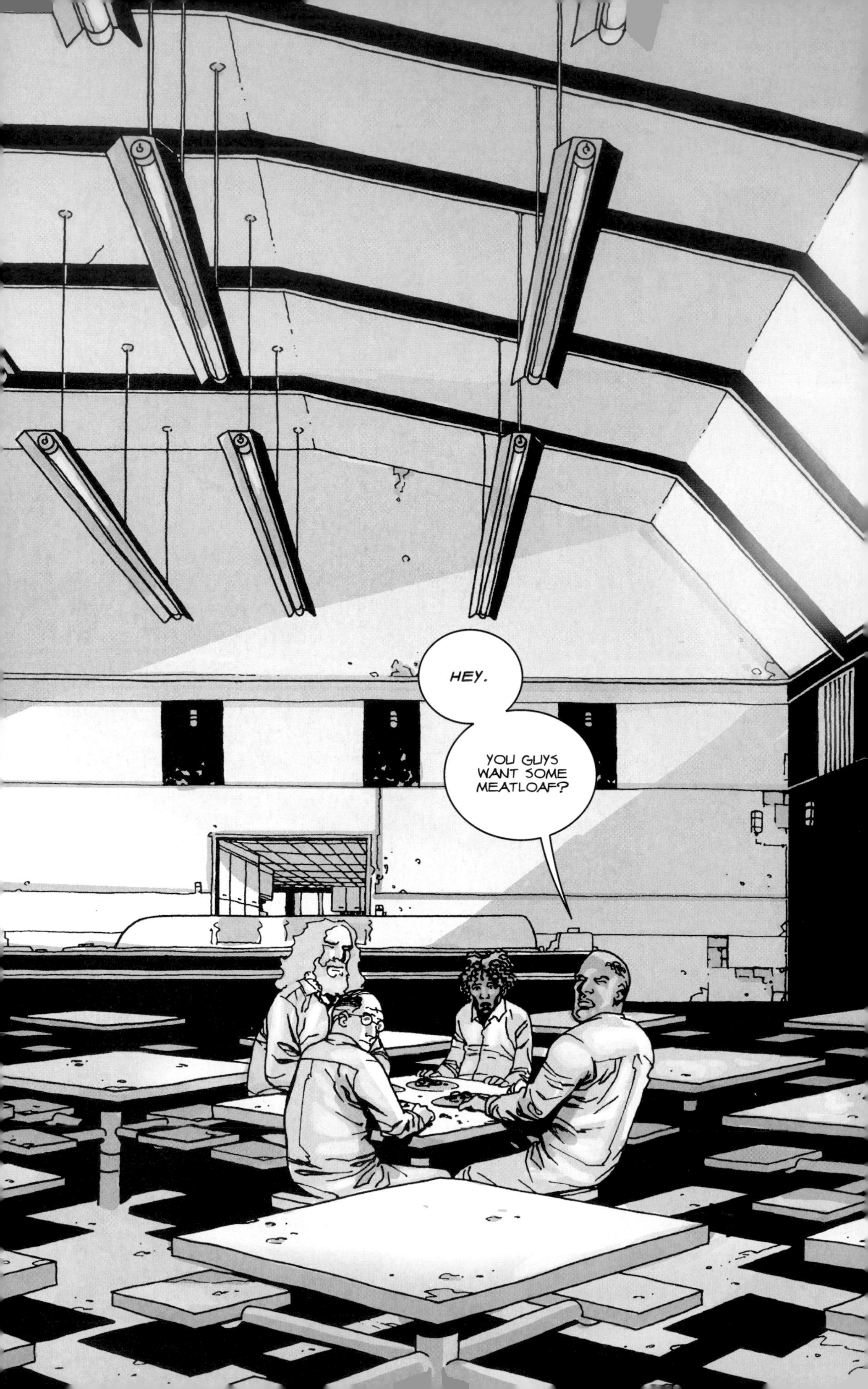
HEY.
YOU GUYS WANT SOME MEATLOAF?

WOW! THIS IS AMAZING.

NOT SURE-- BUT I CAN STILL BE IMPRESSED.

CHANGING YOUR MIND ABOUT THIS PLACE YET? YOU THINK WE CAN STAY HERE?

C'MON, EVERYBODY-- THEY'VE GOT THE FOOD BACK THIS WAY. I KNOW YOU'RE ALL STARVED.

NOT TOO MUCH, SON. WE'VE GOT TO SAVE ENOUGH FOR EVERYONE TO HAVE SOME.

RICK, LOOK AT THIS TRAY. I DON'T THINK WE CAN EAT ALL THIS IF WE TRIED.

I DON'T MEAN TO INTERRUPT--BUT YOU GUYS DON'T LOOK LIKE NO RESCUE TEAM TO ME. I MEAN YOU ACT LIKE YOU AIN'T EATEN IN WEEKS.

YOU FOLLOW ME?

RESCUE TEAM? NO--WE'RE JUST...I DON'T KNOW WHAT WE ARE... WE'RE JUST PEOPLE. YOU GUYS ARE DOING MUCH BETTER IN HERE THAN WE WERE OUT THERE.

WE'RE NOT HERE TO RESCUE YOU.

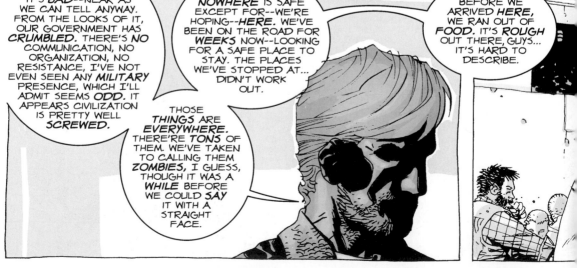

IT'S BAD--NEAR AS WE CAN TELL ANYWAY. FROM THE LOOKS OF IT, OUR GOVERNMENT HAS CRUMBLED. THERE'S NO COMMUNICATION, NO ORGANIZATION, NO RESISTANCE, I'VE NOT EVEN SEEN ANY MILITARY PRESENCE, WHICH I'LL ADMIT SEEMS ODD. IT APPEARS CIVILIZATION IS PRETTY WELL SCREWED.

NOWHERE IS SAFE EXCEPT FOR--WE'RE HOPING--HERE. WE'VE BEEN ON THE ROAD FOR WEEKS NOW--LOOKING FOR A SAFE PLACE TO STAY. THE PLACES WE'VE STOPPED AT... DIDN'T WORK OUT.

THOSE THINGS ARE EVERYWHERE. THERE'RE TONS OF THEM. WE'VE TAKEN TO CALLING THEM ZOMBIES, I GUESS, THOUGH IT WAS A WHILE BEFORE WE COULD SAY IT WITH A STRAIGHT FACE.

BEFORE WE ARRIVED HERE, WE RAN OUT OF FOOD. IT'S ROUGH OUT THERE, GUYS... IT'S HARD TO DESCRIBE.

NICE.

HM.

HOW BAD *IS* IT OUT THERE?

WHAT DO YOU *MEAN?*

WE SAW THE REPORTS ON *TV*--AND THEN ALL *HELL* BROKE LOOSE IN *HERE.* SINCE THEN WE'VE BEEN HOLED UP IN HERE, WITH *NO* WORD FROM THE OUTSIDE WORLD. WE DON'T KNOW *WHAT'S* GOING ON.

YOU GUYS *MIGHT* WANT TO *SIT DOWN.*

WAIT A MINUTE--YOU GUYS *ARE* GUARDS-- *AREN'T* YOU?

OH, THAT'S *RICH*.

DO WE *LOOK* LIKE PRISON GUARDS TO *YOU*?

NO--I SUPPOSE *NOT*.

ALLEN, KEEP AN *EYE* ON *CARL*.

YOU'RE *INMATES*? PRISON *INMATES*?! WHAT DID YOU *DO*? WHAT *CRIMES* DID YOU COMMIT?

ARMED ROBBERY.

TAX FRAUD--BUT IT WASN'T *MY* FAULT.

DRUGS, MAN-- POSESSION, SELLING, STEALING... I'VE DONE IT *ALL*. BUT I'M *CLEAN* NOW-- *TOTALLY* CLEAN... GOTTA BE, Y'KNOW...

MURDER.

MURDER?

YEAH, AND I KNOW WHAT YOU'RE *THINKING*, BUT YOU GOT *NOTHING* TO WORRY ABOUT UNLESS YOU'RE MY *WIFE* OR HER *BOYFRIEND*. AND YOU *CAN'T* BE THEM, BECAUSE THEY'RE *DEAD*.

SO *RELAX*. BESIDES-- THE ONE YOU *SHOULD* BE WORRIED ABOUT IS *ANDREW* HERE.

WHY'S THAT?

HE'S THE ONE THAT *CAUSED* THIS WHOLE *LIVING DEAD* SHIT.

TELL 'EM, ANDREW.

UH-- *YEAH*... IT'S UH... IT'S LIKE *THIS*, SEE? I WAS A HARDCORE USER--

HARDCORE.

I WAS A REPEAT OFFENDER-- Y'KNOW? I WAS HERE FOR MY *SECOND* TIME...

MY LIFE WAS A *WRECK*--ALL BECAUSE A' MY *ADDICTION*. I COULDN'T FUNCTION, Y'KNOW... I WAS HERE-- *AGAIN*...I DIDN'T KNOW WHAT *ELSE* TO DO.

SO I TURNED TO *GOD*--IF YOU CAN BELIEVE IT. I ASKED HIM--*BEGGED HIM*-- TO PLEASE, HELP GET ME OFF THAT SMACK. I WANTED TO GO CLEAN, ONCE AND FOR ALL... I KNEW I WOULDN'T BE ABLE TO DO IT WITHOUT *HIS* HELP.

SO I *ASKED* HIM--AND THE *NEXT DAY* THE NEWS REPORTS STARTED.

NOW LOOK AT ME. I'M COMPLETELY CLEAN. I COULDN'T-- I COULDN'T GET MY HANDS ON ANYTHING IF I *TRIED*.

GYM'S UP *THIS* WAY.

LEAD THE WAY--BUT KEEP YOUR *EYES* OPEN. THEY DON'T MOVE VERY *FAST* BUT THEY COULD STILL BE *ANYWHERE.*

BE A LITTLE *EASIER* IF I HAD ONE OF *THOSE.* YOU GONNA GIVE ME A GUN?

WAY I FIGURE IT--IF YOU'RE A DECENT MAN YOU WON'T MIND *PROVIN'* IT.

AND *YOU?* I DON'T KNOW *SHIT* ABOUT YOU PEOPLE.

WE HAVEN'T SHOT YOU *YET*--SO YOU'RE JUST GOING TO HAVE TO *TRUST* US.

WHATEVER-- LIKE I GOT A *CHOICE.*

THIS IS *IT,* BUT SOMEBODY'S CUFFED THE *DOORS* CLOSED.

WHOEVER IT WAS LEFT THE *KEY* IN THEM SO THEY COULD BE UNLOCKED.

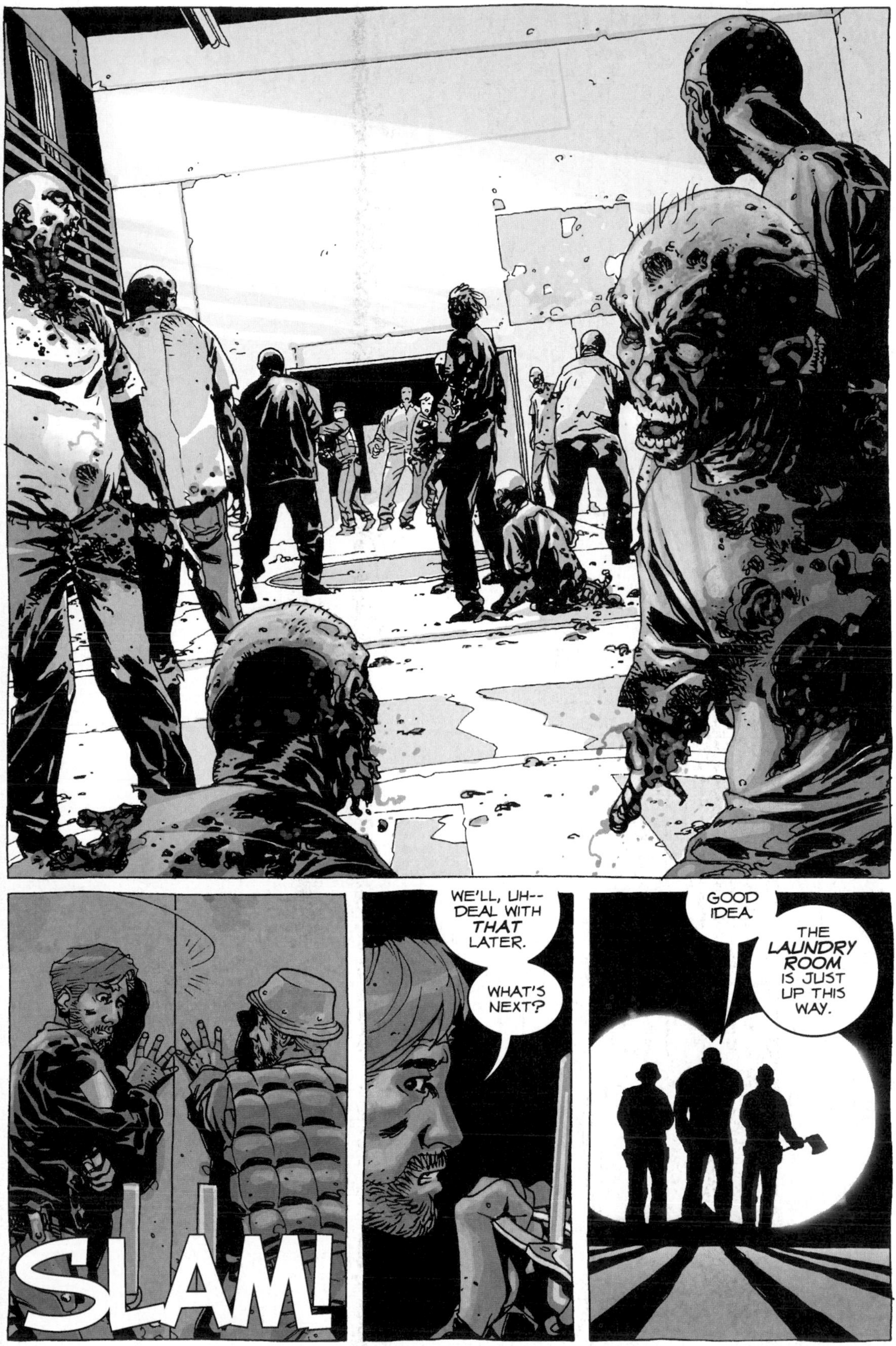
SLAM!
WE'LL, UH-- DEAL WITH THAT LATER.
WHAT'S NEXT?
GOOD IDEA.
THE LAUNDRY ROOM IS JUST UP THIS WAY.

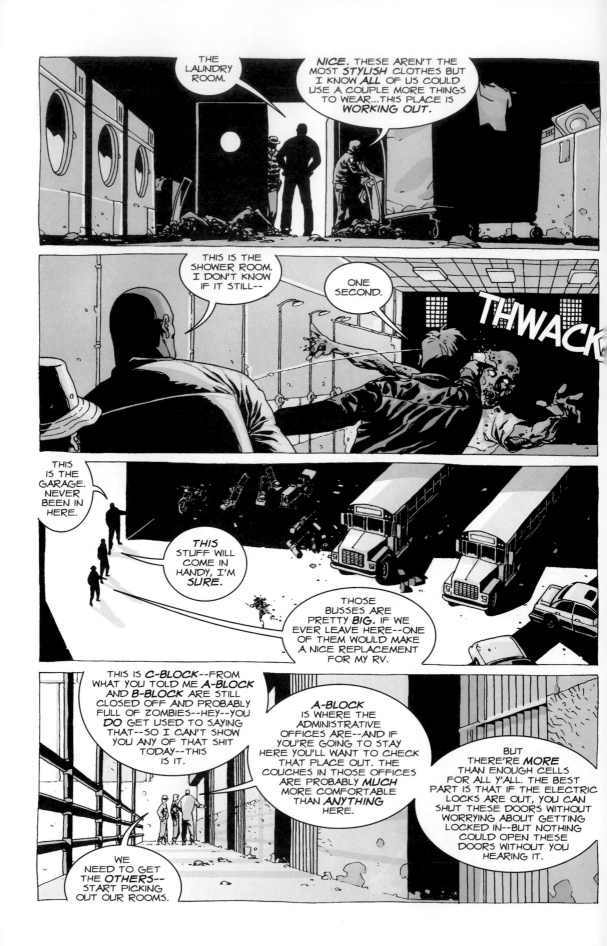

...OH, THAT *AXEL* GUY SEEMED *NICE.*

I DON'T *CARE*--I'M JUST GLAD THEY'RE SLEEPING ON THE *LOWER* LEVEL. I *LIKE* THAT THEY DON'T TRUST US AS MUCH AS *WE* DON'T TRUST THEM...

NO WAY, RICK. WHY WOULD YOU EVEN *SUGGEST* SUCH A THING?

I'M THINKING *LONG-TERM* HERE, *TYREESE.* THIS MAKES *SENSE* IF WE'RE GOING TO BE *STAYING* HERE. I DON'T *CARE* WHAT HE DID--AND IF *I* DON'T CARE, I DON'T SEE WHY *YOU* WOULD.

THAT MAN WAS GOING TO *KILL* YOU! HE'S DANGEROUS!

WHAT ARE YOU ARGUING ABOUT?

LOOK AT THE CIRCUMSTANCES, MAN... HE JUST LOST HIS *KIDS*--!

RICK WANTS TO GO GET *HERSHEL* AND EVERYONE AT HIS *FARM*--BRING THEM *HERE* TO LIVE.

I MISS *GLENN* AS MUCH AS *ANYONE* BUT YOU *CAN'T* BRING THEM *HERE!* HERSHEL WAS *CRAZY.*

HERSHEL HAD A *LOT* GOING ON. BUT HE'S A FARMER--WE *NEED* HIM. HE COULD PLOW UP SOME OF THOSE *FIELDS* OUT THERE AND WE COULD GROW FOOD *INSIDE* THE FENCE.

IT'S *SAFER* HERE ANYWAY--I DON'T THINK IT'S *RIGHT* TO JUST LEAVE HIM MILES AWAY KNOWING WE'VE GOT PLENTY OF *ROOM* IN HERE.

WITH GLENN, OTIS, PATRICIA, AND HERSHEL AND HIS KIDS WE COULD CLEAN THIS PLACE UP IN *NO TIME.* WE OPEN THOSE OTHER WINGS OF THE PRISON AND WE'LL HAVE *PLENTY* OF ROOM FOR ANYONE WHO STUMBLED UPON THIS PLACE.

WITH HERSHEL HERE GROWING FOOD AND TEACHING US TO *FARM* WE COULD MAKE A *LIFE* HERE-- LONG-TERM.

THIS MAKES SENSE, GUYS. *TRUST* ME.

I SAW *GAS* IN THE GARAGE TODAY... I THINK DALE AND I SHOULD TAKE THE *RV* OVER THERE *TOMORROW.* IT WOULDN'T TAKE THAT LONG SINCE THE ROAD IS ALREADY *CLEARED OFF.*

LET *ME* TALK TO HIM. I THINK IT'D BE LESS *THREATENING* IF I GO UP THERE *ALONE*. I DON'T WANT TO STARTLE HIM--I GOT NO *CLUE* WHAT FRAME OF MIND HE'S IN.

OKAY-- I'LL WAIT *HERE.* I JUST HOPE YOU KNOW WHAT YOU'RE *DOING.*

OH, GOD.

RICK!

WHAT *HAPPENED* HERE? WAS THERE ANOTHER *ATTACK?*

A *FEW,* ACTUALLY. WE'RE GETTING ATTACKED A *LOT* MORE OFTEN NOW, IT SEEMS. I THINK THE *COLD* WAS SLOWING THEM DOWN, BUT IT'S GOING TO BE *SPRING* SOON.

THINGS'RE JUST *WORSE.*

THEN IT LOOKS LIKE I CAME AT THE RIGHT *TIME.* THERE'S AN ABANDONED PRISON--JUST A FEW *HOURS* DRIVE FROM HERE. WE'VE ALREADY CLEANED OUT A PORTION OF IT AND MADE IT *LIVEABLE.* THERE'S ENOUGH ROOM FOR EVERYONE HERE AND *MORE.* IT'S GOT A BETTER FENCE SYSTEM THAN THIS PLACE--AND MORE LAND *INSIDE* THE FENCE.

YOU'RE *ALL* WELCOME TO PACK UP AND LIVE THERE *WITH US.* DALE IS UP ON THE ROAD IN THE *RV,* WE COULD ALL PACK INTO THAT THING AND *GO.* YOU COULDN'T TAKE *EVERYTHING* NOW AND WE'LL STILL HAVE TO FIGURE OUT SOMETHING FOR THE *LIVESTOCK,* BUT YOU COULD COME BACK TO GET MOST OF YOUR STUFF TOMORROW OR *LATER.* THIS PLACE IS *COMPLETELY* SAFE.

IF WE LEAVE *SOON*--WE COULD BE THERE BEFORE *DARK.*

THAT--

THAT MAKES A WHOLE LOT OF SENSE.

HAVE ANY TROUBLE HOLDING DOWN THE *FORT* IN MY ABSENCE?

OH MY GOD. I *LIVE* IN A *FORT.* MY TEN YEAR-OLD SELF WOULD HAVE THE BIGGEST *BONER* OVER LIVING IN THIS PLACE.

HEH.

YEAH, IT'S OKAY. WE MADE SURE THE PRISON GROUNDS ARE *SECURE.* WE DOUBLE CHECKED ALL THE OUTER DOORS TO THE PRISON WINGS WE *HAVEN'T* CLEARED YET. EVERYTHING'S GOING WELL.

IT TOOK A *WHILE* TO FINISH DRAGGING THESE BODIES OUT TO *BURN* BUT WE'RE DONE *NOW.*

WE DIDN'T GET AROUND TO THE *GYM,* THOUGH. THAT'S SOMETHING WE'LL HAVE TO DO TOMORROW.

EVERYONE SETTLING IN OKAY?

LORI'S NOT HAPPY WITH OUR NEW *ROOMMATES.* YOU'LL PROBABLY HEAR ABOUT IT LATER. *AXEL* HELPED ME DRAG SOME OF THE BODIES OUT HERE AND *THOMAS,* THE KINDA *NERDY* GUY, HAS BEEN HELPING THE WOMEN MOVE ALL THEIR BELONGINGS INTO THE CELLS AND MOVE *BEDS* AROUND AND STUFF. ANDREW AND DEXTER KINDA KEPT TO *THEMSELVES,* SETTING UP THEIR CELLS AND STUFF.

THEY'RE *OKAY* IN *MY* BOOK.

THAT'S GOOD TO KNOW.

OH, AND I THINK I SAW *ALLEN* SMILING EARLIER TODAY. THIS PLACE SEEMS TO REALLY BE LIFTING *HIS* SPIRITS.

IT SURE DOES MAKE RAISING KIDS IN THIS *HELL* SEEM A *LITTLE* MORE POSSIBLE. I HAVEN'T FELT *THIS* OPTIMISTIC SINCE WE FIRST ARRIVED AT WILSHIRE ESTATES.

WHICH I *GUESS* SHOULD *PROBABLY* WORRY ME.

I THINK THESE BEDS WILL REALLY WORK OUT.

THROWING *EXTRA* MATTRESSES OVER THESE TWIN BEDS SIDEWAYS TO MAKE THEM ONE *BIG* BED WAS *BRILLIANT.* HOPEFULLY THEY'LL BE A LITTLE SOFTER WITH THE EXTRA PADDING. IT WAS A STEP UP FROM THE RV COUCH LAST NIGHT--BUT STILL NOT SOMETHING I'D WANT TO SLEEP ON FOREVER.

AM I FAT?

YEAH, *OF COURSE* YOU'RE FAT...YOU'RE *PREGNANT.* OR HAVE YOU FORGOTTEN?

I KNOW--I JUST DON'T REMEMBER SHOWING *THIS* MUCH *THIS* EARLY...

I MEAN, IF *ANDREA* IS KEEPING TRACK OF THE DAYS RIGHT--I'M BARELY *HALF*-WAY THROUGH THIS.

MAYBE YOU'RE *FURTHER* ALONG THAN YOU THOUGHT... WHAT IF YOU'RE STARTING YOUR COUNT ON THE *WRONG* DAY?

ER...

WHERE'S TYREESE AT? IT'S GETTING KINDA *LATE* ISN'T IT?

HE'S OUT LOOKING FOR CHRIS AND JULIE... HE THINKS THEY RAN OFF TO... Y'KNOW. NOBODY'S SEEN THEM FOR AT *LEAST* AN HOUR.

YOU GOT A MINUTE?

I GOT A *FEW*.

I JUST WANTED TO *THANK* YOU FOR--

IT'S NOT *NECESSARY*, HERSHEL. YOU DON'T HAVE TO--

LET ME *TALK*. I WANTED TO THANK YOU FOR *BRINGING* US HERE, RICK. I KNOW THINGS BETWEEN US--

I *WAS* GOING TO *SHOOT* YOU, RICK.

I THINK IT'S ONLY FAIR THAT YOU *KNOW* THAT. I *WOULD* HAVE KILLED YOU. I WAS OUT OF MY *MIND* WITH *GRIEF*. I *STILL* DON'T KNOW IF I'M BACK TO NORMAL. I JUST--I HAVEN'T TOUCHED A GUN SINCE THAT DAY, RICK... AND I DON'T PLAN TO--*EVER AGAIN*.

THIS *PLACE*--IT'S *SPECIAL*, RICK. IT'S GOING TO BE A NEW *LIFE* FOR ME, MY *KIDS*. THIS IS A NEW *BEGINNING* FOR US. I--THANK YOU, RICK.

IT WAS THE RIGHT THING TO *DO*, HERSHEL. I COULDN'T LEAVE YOU PEOPLE OUT THERE...NOT KNOWING THAT *WE* HAD *THIS* PLACE.

C'MON-- IT'S GETTING *LATE*, AND YOU'RE GOING TO NEED TO START *EARLY* TOMORROW IF YOU'RE GOING TO GET THE REST OF YOUR STUFF FROM YOUR FARM--AND FIGURE OUT WHAT WE'RE GOING TO DO WITH YOUR LIVESTOCK.

EVENTUALLY WE'LL WANT TO KEEP THEM *HERE*. BUT FOR NOW, *OTIS* OFFERED TO STAY THERE AND WATCH THEM. I THINK HE AND *PATRICIA* ARE SPLITTING UP.

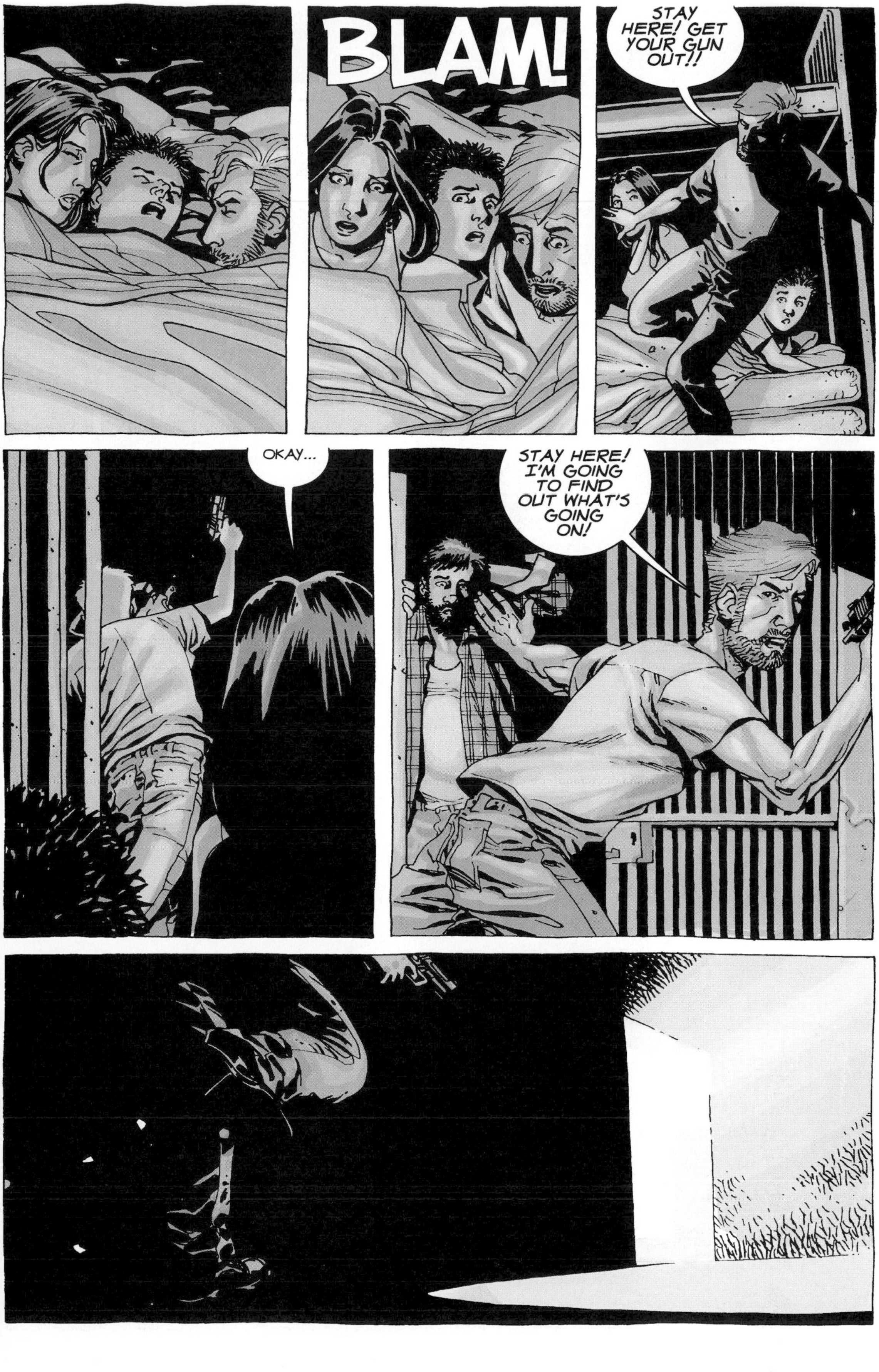
BLAM!
STAY HERE! GET YOUR GUN OUT!!
OKAY...
STAY HERE! I'M GOING TO FIND OUT WHAT'S GOING ON!

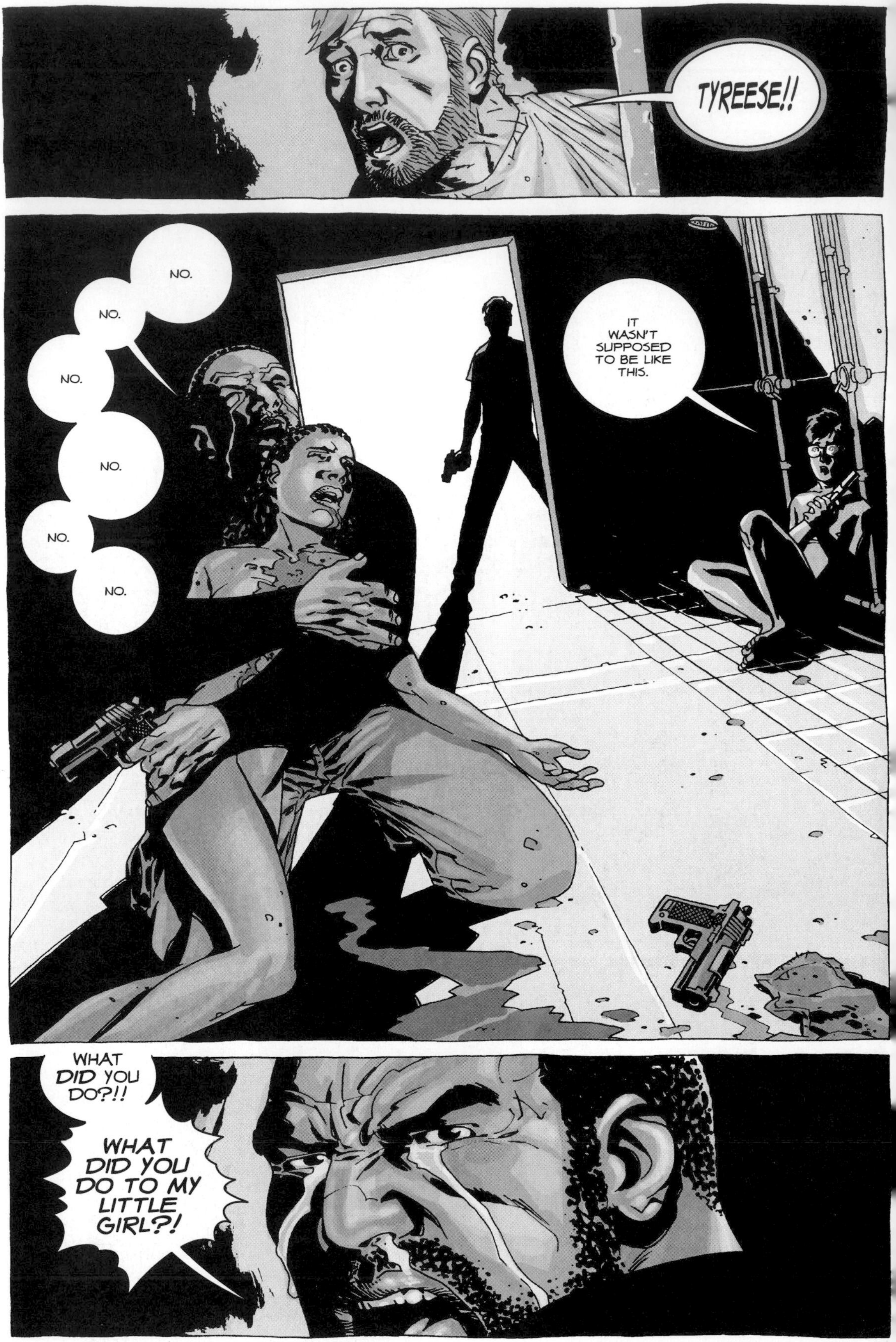
TYREESE!!
NO.
NO.
NO.
NO.
NO.
NO.
IT WASN'T SUPPOSED TO BE LIKE THIS.
WHAT DID YOU DO?!!
WHAT DID YOU DO TO MY LITTLE GIRL?!

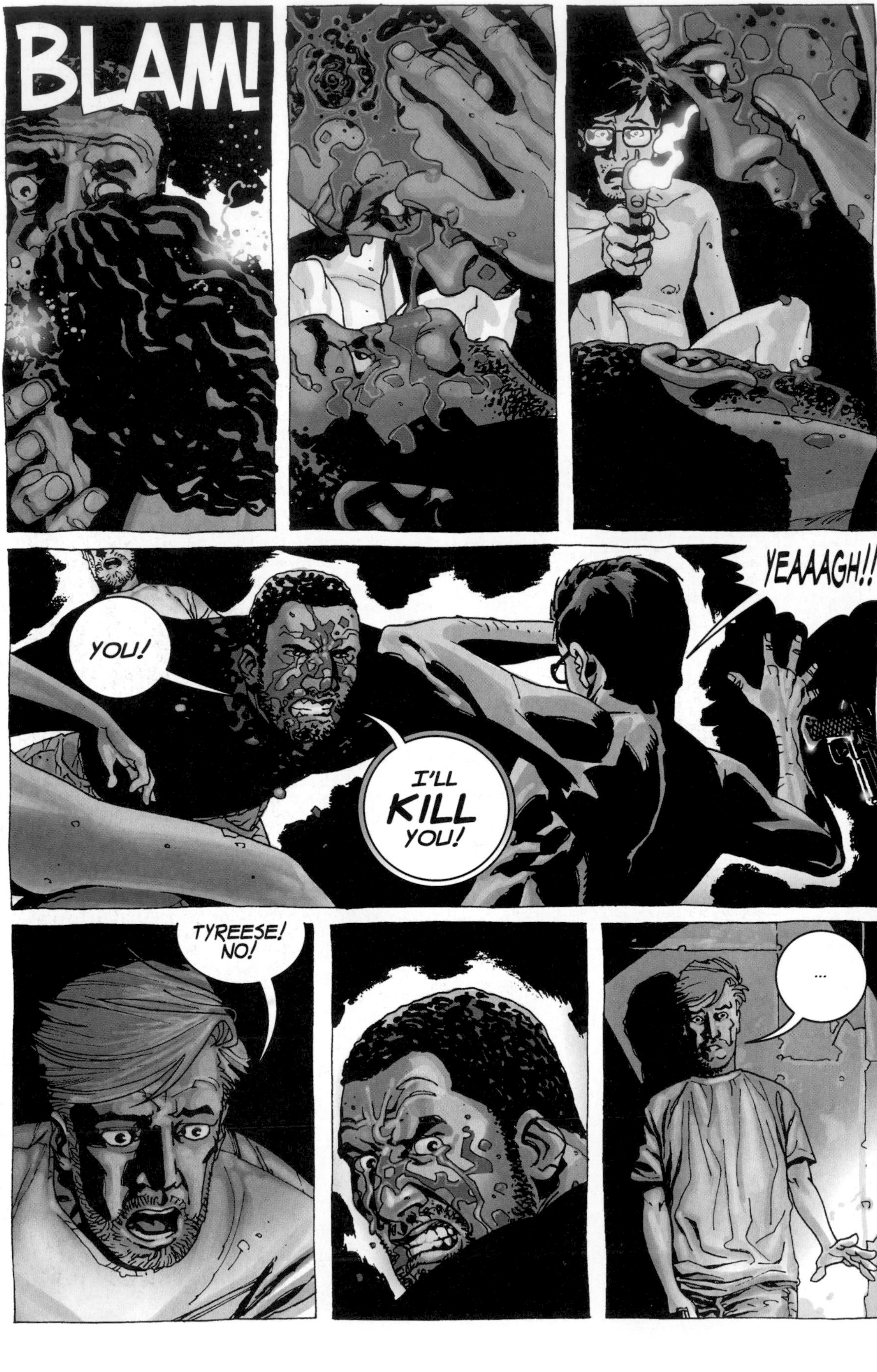
BLAM!
YEAAAGH!!
YOU!
I'LL KILL YOU!
TYREESE! NO!
...

--!

STOP. JUST-- STOP.

HE'S *DEAD,* TYREESE... YOU *KILLED* HIM.

DEAR GOD, MAN-- YOU *KILLED* HIM.

YEAH. LEAVE ME. HE'LL BE COMING BACK SOON, AND I'M GOING TO *KILL* HIM *AGAIN.*

SLOWER THIS TIME.

I'LL *BURN* THEM BOTH TOMORROW-- FIRST THING IN THE MORNING. WE CAN TALK ABOUT THIS *THEN.*

RICK! WHAT HAPPENED? WHAT'S GOING ON?

IT'S--OH, LORI--IT'S HORRIBLE.

CHRIS AND JULIE--THEY *KILLED* EACH OTHER-- SOME SORT OF *SUICIDE PACT.* THEY WERE *CRAZY*--THOUGHT THEY COULD BE TOGETHER *FOREVER* IF THEY DID THIS.

TYREESE IS...*DEALING* WITH IT.

I JUST--I THOUGHT IT *BEST* TO JUST LEAVE HIM *ALONE.*

TYREESE WAS ALREADY THERE WHEN I GOT THERE. HE *FOUND* THEIR *BODIES.* WE WERE--THERE--WHEN THEY *CAME BACK.* THEY WEREN'T *BITTEN,* BUT THEY *DID.*

OH, GOD...

THEY'RE *DEAD?*

YEAH.

THEY'RE *BOTH DEAD.*

I NEED TO *SLEEP.*

WE *ALL* DO.

I WOULD HAVE-- IF YOU HAD SAID *SOMETHING*--I WOULD HAVE *HELPED* YOU. YOU DIDN'T HAVE TO BRING THEM OUT HERE ALL BY *YOURSELF*.

THIS WAS SOMETHING I HAD TO DO *ALONE*.

I TOLD THE OTHERS THAT THEY KILLED *EACH OTHER*, AND THEN THEY BOTH TURNED. I DON'T THINK THEY'D UNDERSTAND.

BUT *I* UNDERSTAND. I WANT YOU TO *KNOW* THAT.

THANK YOU, *RICK*.

C'MON-- LET'S GET BACK. THERE'S A *LOT* TO DO TODAY.

TYREESE, I DO NOT EXPECT YOU TO DO ANY--

ARE YOU ALL RIGHT?

I'M *FINE*, RICK.

REALLY.

IS HE--?

HE'S ACTING AS THOUGH *NOTHING* HAPPENED, LORI. IT'S VERY-- UNSETTLING.

HE JUST *SMILED* AT ME. HE LOOKED AT ME AND HE *SMILED.*

I'M WORRIED ABOUT HIM. ALLEN WAS ONE THING--BUT FOR TYREESE TO BE SHOWING NO EMOTION WHATSOEVER... IT MAKES ME WORRY.

KEEP AN *EYE* ON HIM FOR ME--TODAY AND TOMORROW. JUST WATCH HIM, MAKE SURE HE DOESN'T DO ANYTHING *DANGEROUS.*

ME? WHAT ARE *YOU* GOING TO BE DOING? YOU ACT AS THOUGH YOU'RE *LEAVING.*

RICK! YOU'RE NOT--!

LORI, *CALM DOWN.* I--

HEY, GUYS. WHAT'S THIS I'M HEARING ABOUT SOME KIDS *DYING* LAST NIGHT? ANDREW SAID HE HEARD SOME SHOTS FIRED LAST NIGHT-- BUT THE *REST* OF US SLEPT RIGHT THROUGH THEM.

TYREESE'S DAUGHTER AND HER BOYFRIEND *KILLED* EACH OTHER LAST NIGHT.

THING IS--THEY BOTH *CAME BACK*--ZOMBIES. BUT NEITHER WERE *BITTEN.*

TYREESE. HE'S THE *BLACK DUDE,* RIGHT? *SHAME.* HIS DAUGHTER WAS *PRETTY.* DIDN'T TRUST THAT BOY, THOUGH. HAD AN *ODD LOOK* TO HIM.

HMPH. I'LL TELL THE OTHERS.

KEEP AN EYE ON *THEM* TOO.

ALWAYS.

C'MON.

WHERE IS HE GOING?

I DON'T KNOW.

WHAT ARE YOU DOING WITH THOSE?

I'M GOING TO TAKE A LOOK AT THOSE OUTER FENCES-- SEE IF I CAN'T GET THEM BACK INTO WORKING ORDER.

GOOD LUCK.

THANKS.

IS HE BEHAVING HIMSELF?

YEAH-- THEY'RE GETTING ALONG LIKE A HOUSE ON FIRE.

AS USUAL.

HAVE YOU TALKED TO HIM?

I SUPPOSE THAT'S BEST.

TYREESE? NO. I WOULDN'T KNOW WHAT TO SAY. ALL I CAN THINK TO DO IS GIVE HIM SOME SPACE.

I DON'T BELIEVE WE'VE MET.

PATRICIA. NICE TO MEET YOU.

THOMAS. I SAW YOU WITH THAT RED-HEADED GUY, OTIS, I THINK HIS NAME WAS...HE YOUR BOYFRIEND?

YEAH, HE-- HE WAS. NOT ANYMORE, THOUGH. WE BROKE UP.

WHAT WAS YOUR NAME AGAIN?

THOMAS. THOMAS RICHARDS.

I CAN'T *BELIEVE* WE GOT STUCK WITH A ROOM RIGHT NEXT TO MY *DAD.*

I'M SURE THAT WAS *HIS* DOING. I DON'T BLAME THE MAN, REALLY. HE STILL BARELY EVEN *KNOWS* ME.

YEAH, BUT THESE ROOMS HAVE *OPEN WALLS.* HE CAN HEAR EVERY WORD WE SAY IN THERE--AMONG *OTHER* THINGS THAT WOULD GO ON IN THAT ROOM.

EH-- I'M NOT SO SURE HE CAN HEAR *EVERYTHING.*

STILL, I KNOW THIS PLACE IS *SAFER*-- AND IT'S *SMARTER* TO LIVE HERE...BUT I *REALLY* MISS MY ROOM, OUR HOUSE...*THE FARM* IN GENERAL.

I'M MORE THAN A LITTLE SHOCKED THAT HE'S LETTING US *SHARE* A ROOM. THAT'S PRETTY *COOL* OF HIM TO DO.

NO IT'S *NOT.* I'M AN *ADULT...* HE NEEDS TO *REALIZE* THAT. I ROOMED WITH A GUY IN COLLEGE. I'M SURE IN HIS MIND WE'RE JUST ROOMMATES.

SUITS ME JUST *FINE.* AS LONG AS WE CAN BE *TOGETHER* I DON'T *CARE* WHAT HE HAS TO TELL HIMSELF.

COLLEGE, HUH? I DIDN'T KNOW THAT.

ONE MEASLY SEMESTER. WE KINDA RAN OUT OF *MONEY* AROUND THE SAME TIME I FLUNKED OUT. I USUALLY PICK THE REASON BASED ON HOW WELL I *KNOW* THE PERSON.

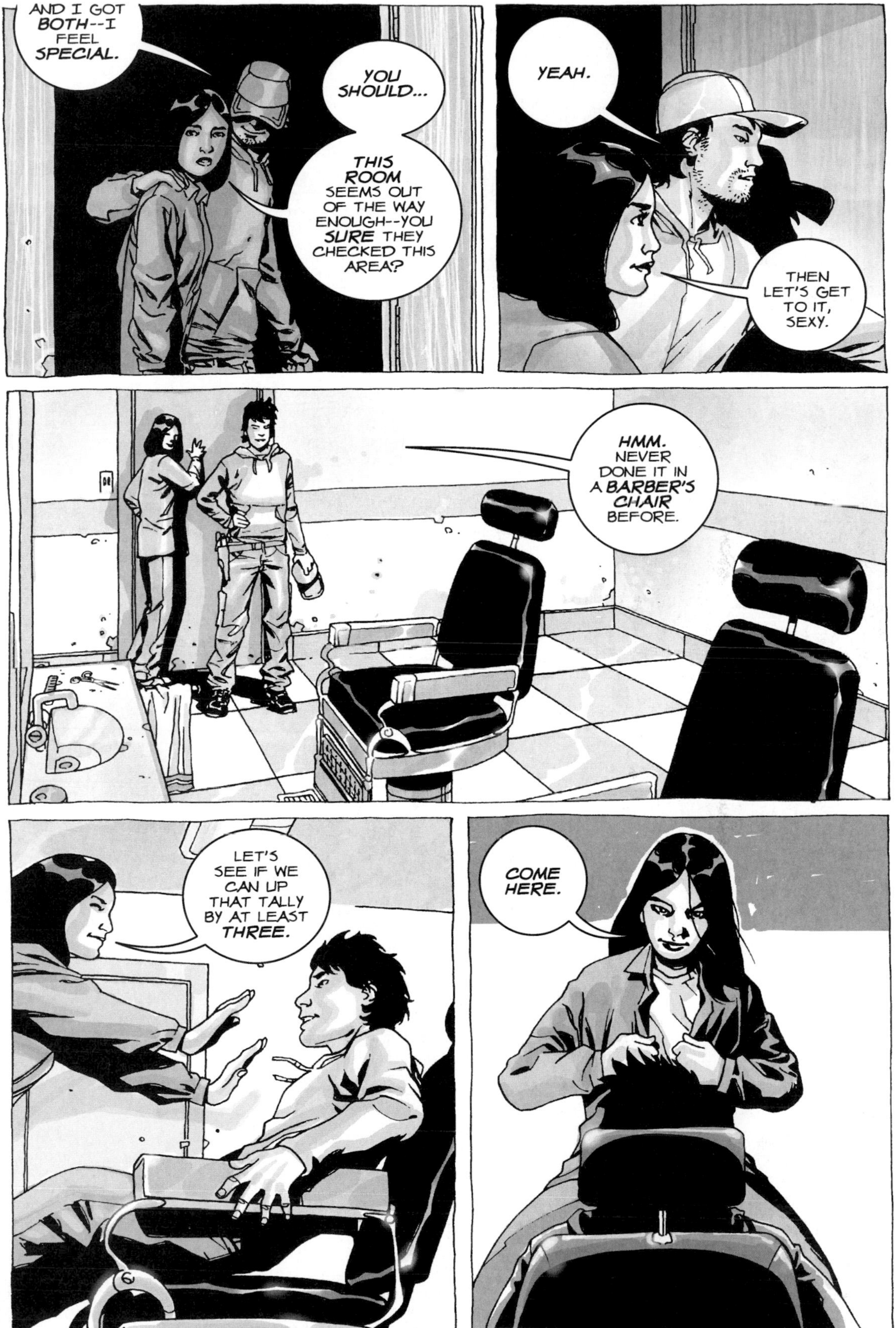
AND I GOT BOTH--I FEEL SPECIAL.
YOU SHOULD...
THIS ROOM SEEMS OUT OF THE WAY ENOUGH--YOU SURE THEY CHECKED THIS AREA?
YEAH.
THEN LET'S GET TO IT, SEXY.
HMM. NEVER DONE IT IN A BARBER'S CHAIR BEFORE.
LET'S SEE IF WE CAN UP THAT TALLY BY AT LEAST THREE.
COME HERE.

YOUR *DAD* COOL WITH YOU HELPING US?

WHAT--I'M SUPPOSED TO SIT AROUND AND DO NOTHING TO HELP OUT BECAUSE MY *DAD'S* WORRIED ABOUT ME?

WHAT HE DOESN'T KNOW WON'T HURT HIM.

OKAY, WE NEED TO GO IN HERE READY TO *FIRE*. THIS PLACE IS *PACKED* WITH 'EM. THERE'S PROBABLY A FEW RIGHT NEXT TO THE *DOOR*.

I KNOW WE DON'T HAVE MANY *BULLETS* LEFT, SO STAY *CLOSE* TO THE DOOR. IF WE RUN OUT, WE JUST WALK BACK OUT AND LOCK THE DOORS.

UNDERSTOOD?

HERE WE GO.

LET'S CLEAR AN AREA AROUND *US* AND THE *DOOR* FIRST... THEN WORK OUR WAY FORWARD WITHOUT LETTING ANY *PAST* US!

BLAM!

SOUNDS LIKE A *PLAN* TO ME.

BLAM! BLAM!

THROK!

BLAM!

RAARGH!

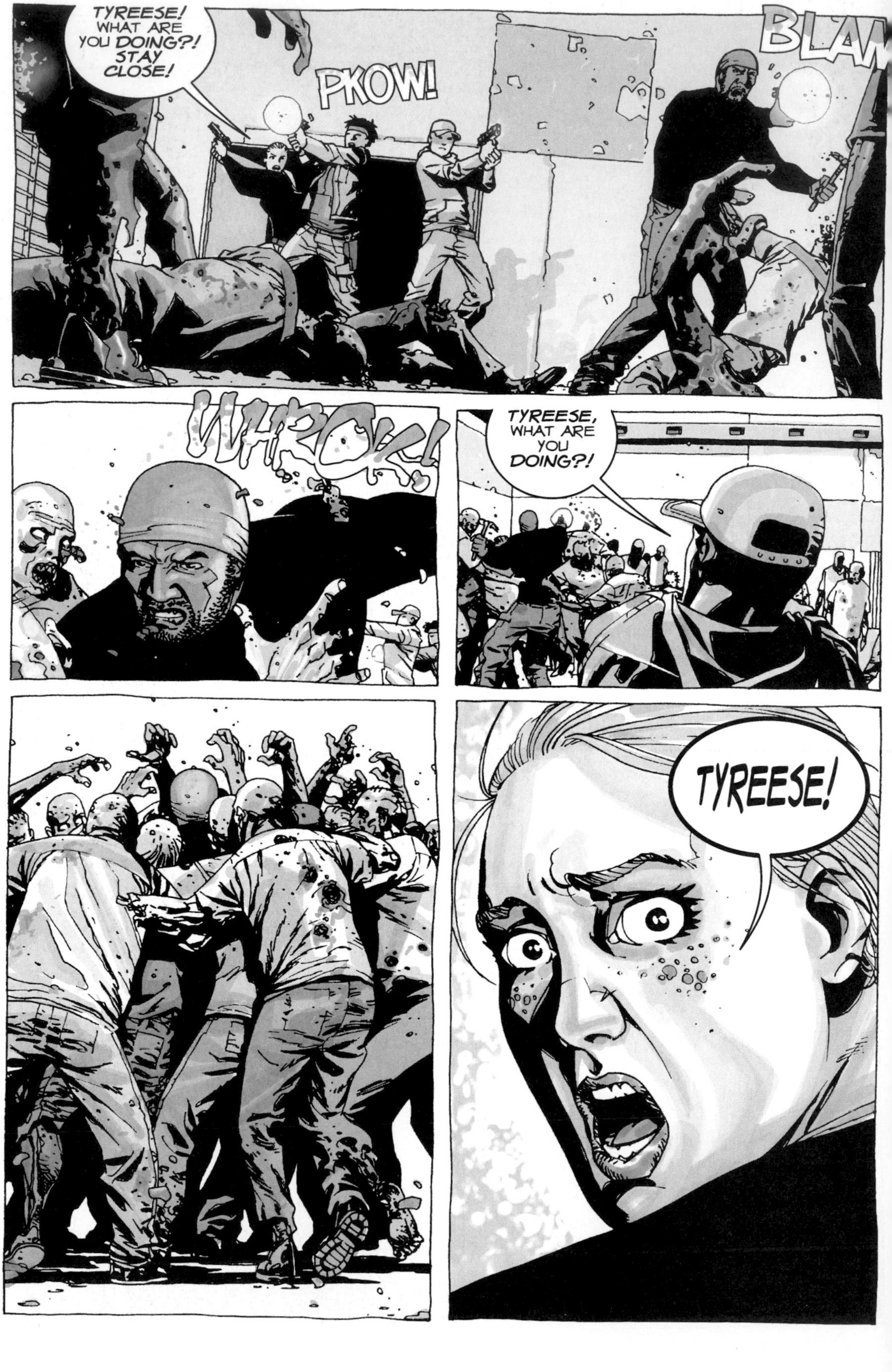
TYREESE! WHAT ARE YOU DOING?! STAY CLOSE!
PKOW!
BLAM
WHACK!
TYREESE, WHAT ARE YOU DOING?!
TYREESE!

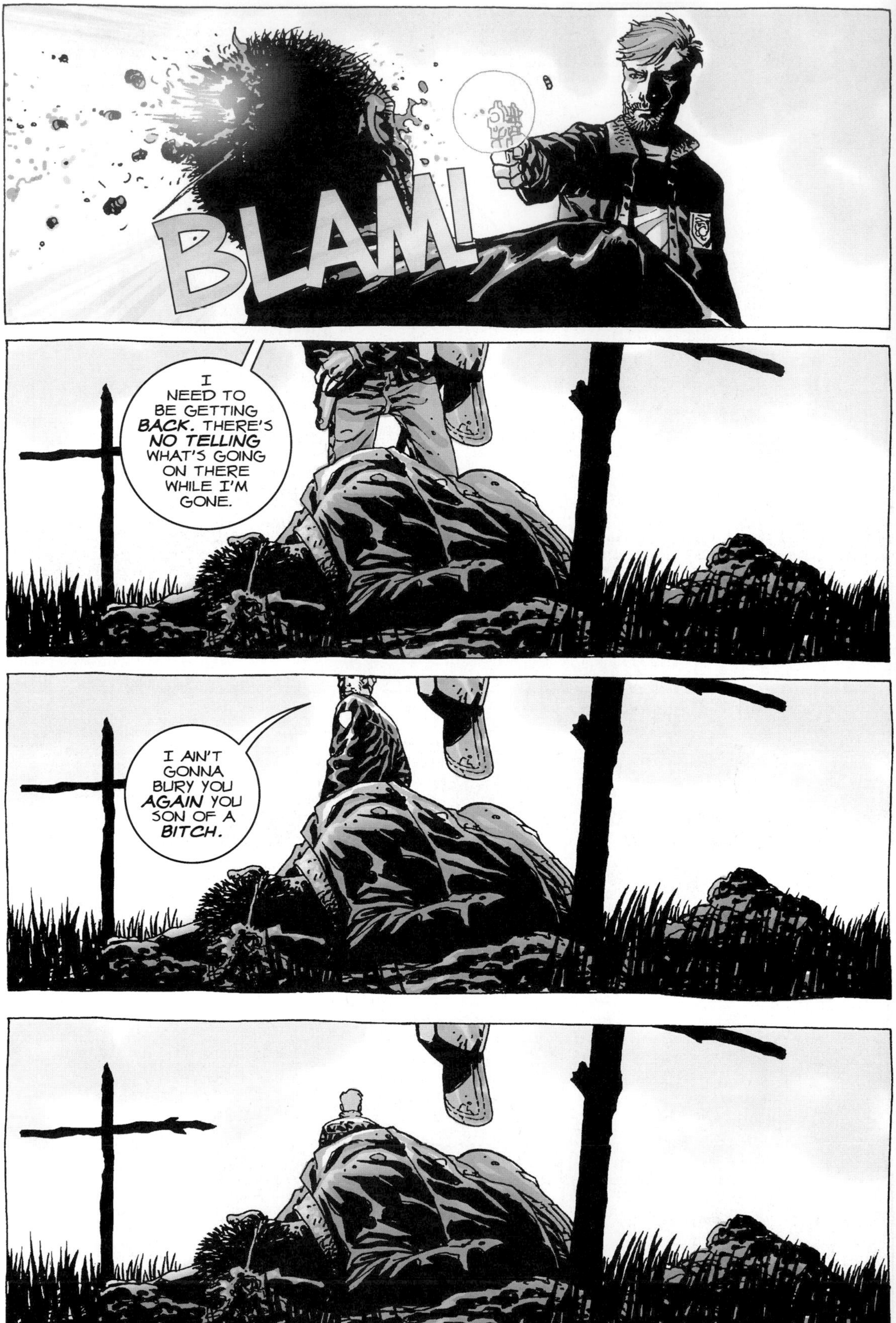
BLAM!
I NEED TO BE GETTING BACK. THERE'S NO TELLING WHAT'S GOING ON THERE WHILE I'M GONE.
I AIN'T GONNA BURY YOU AGAIN YOU SON OF A BITCH.

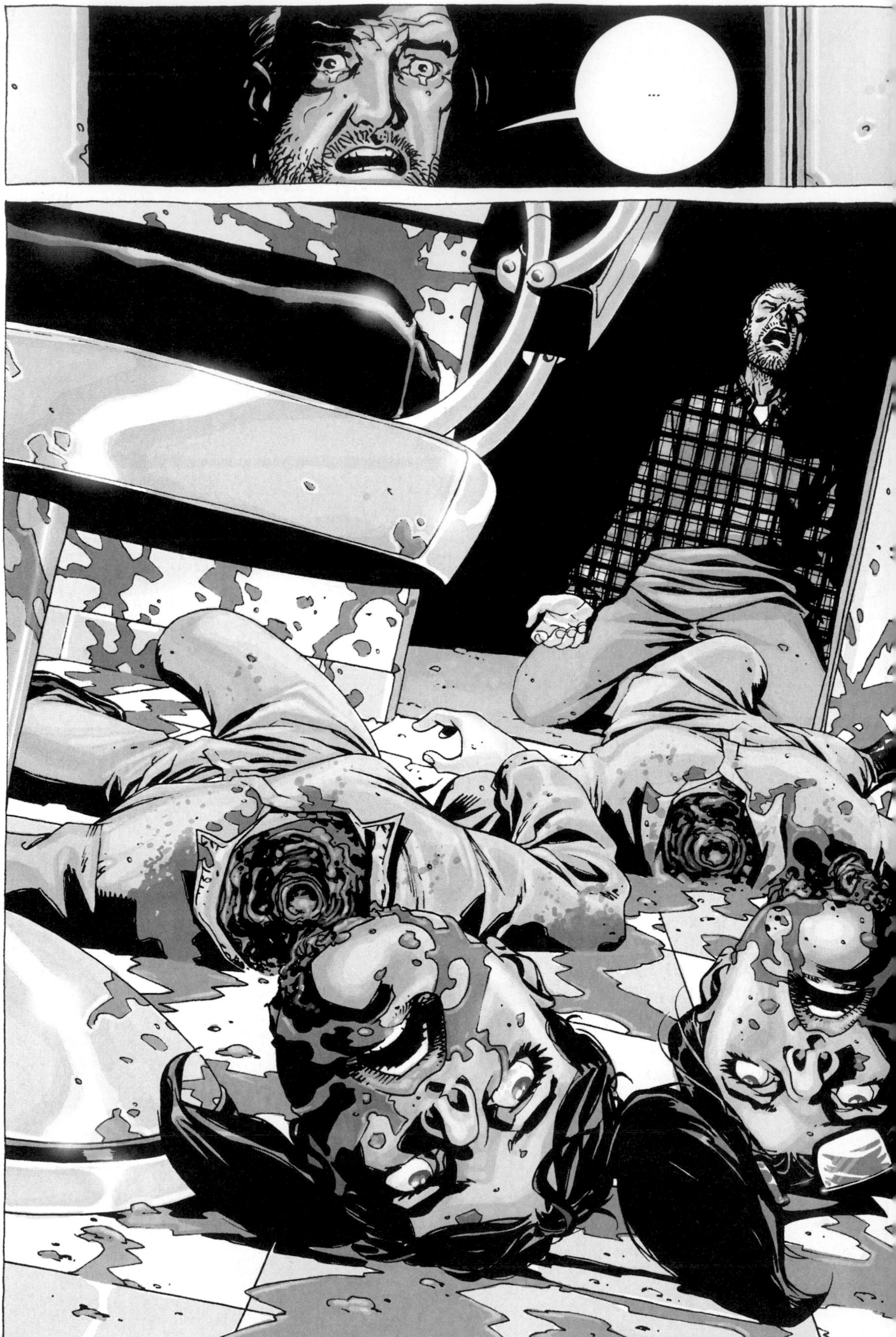
...

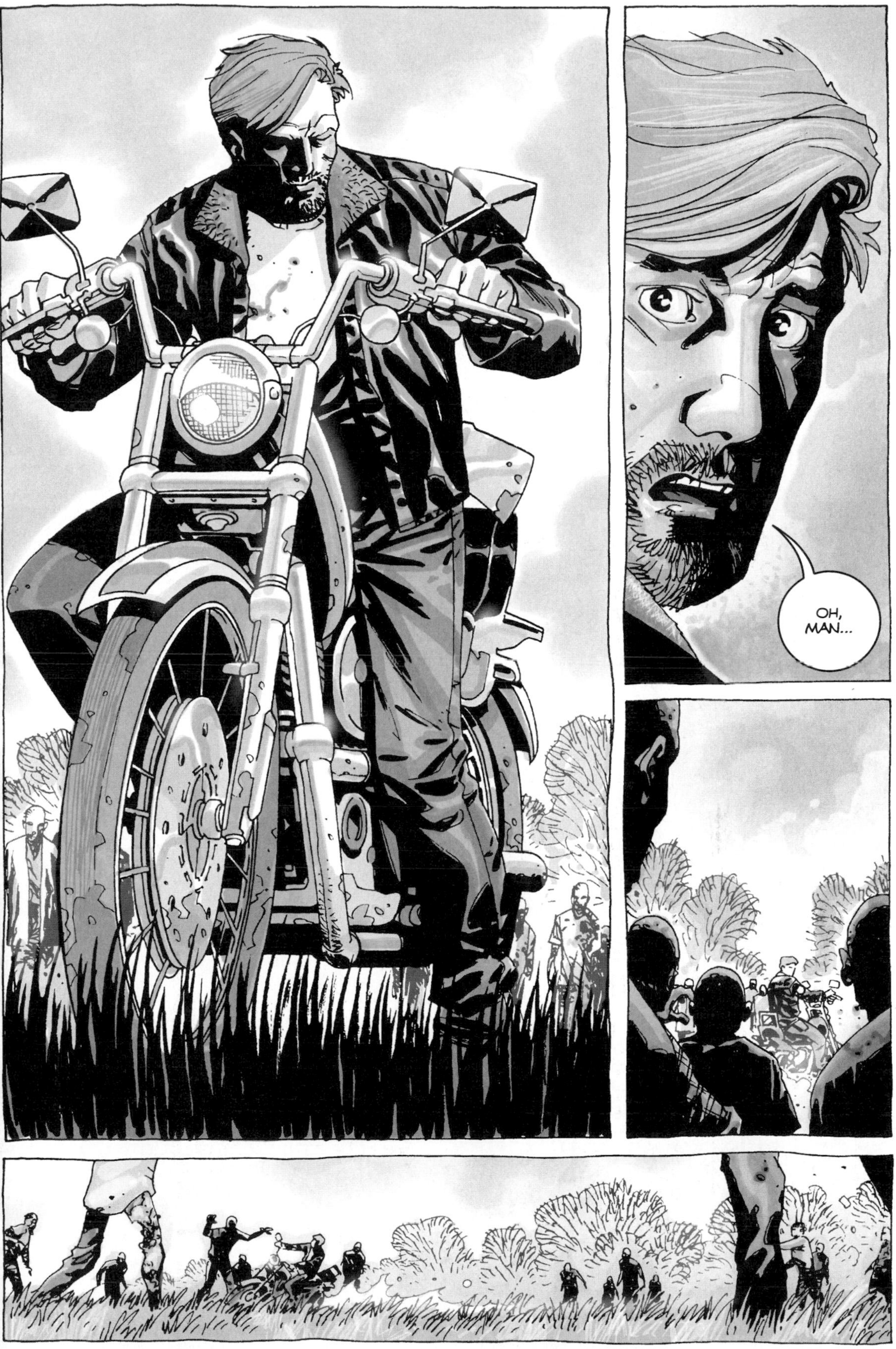
OH, MAN...

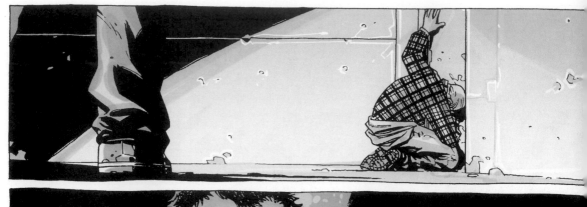

DAD?

WHAT'S WRONG DAD?!

OH, GOD, DAD! WHAT HAPPENED?!

WHAT HAPPENED?!

WHAT IS IT?

OH, GOD!

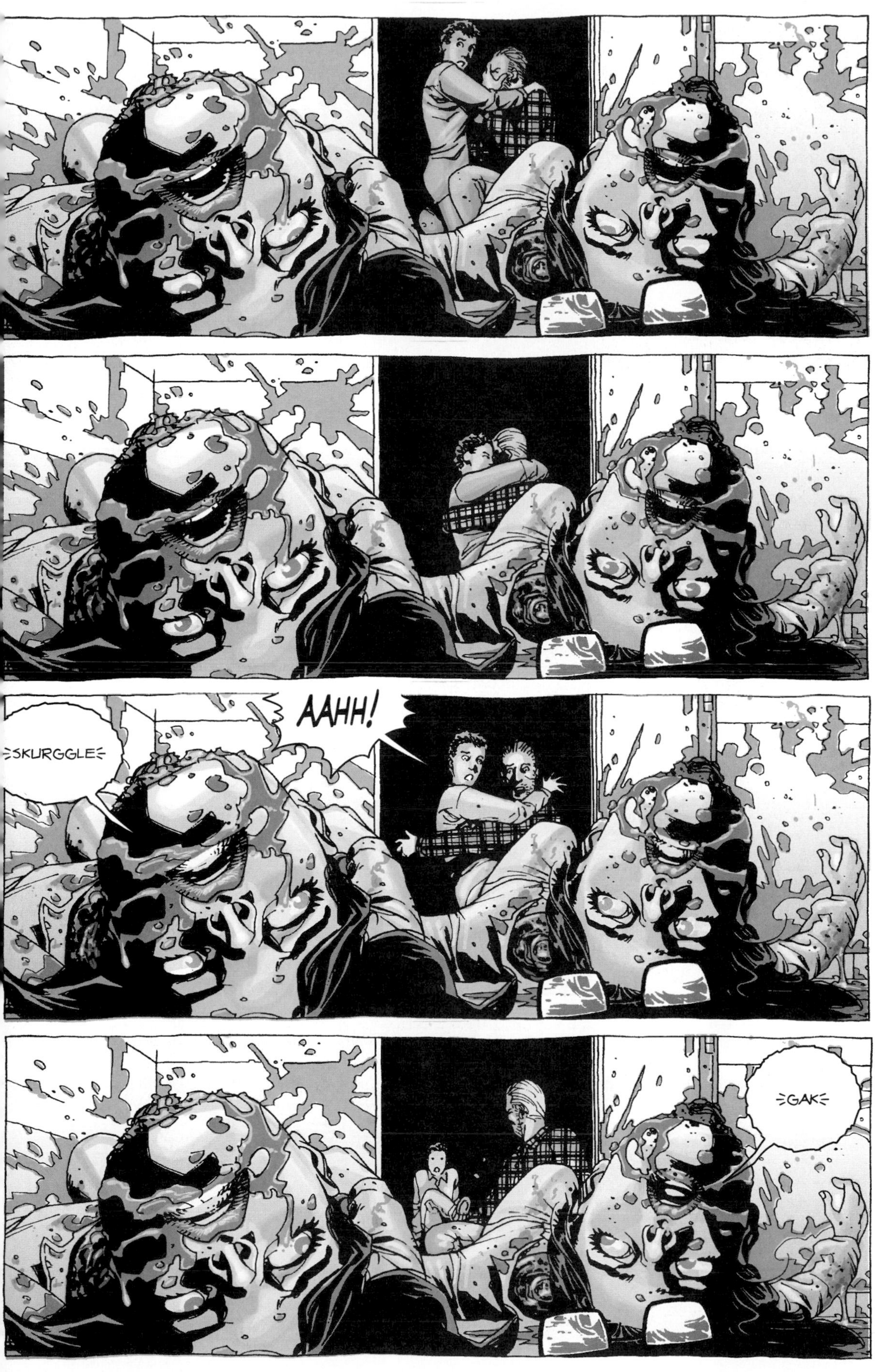

SKURGGLE
AAHH!
GAK

TYREESE!!

ANDREA, NO!

GLENN, GODDAMMIT! LET GO OF ME!

NO! ALL YOU'RE GOING TO DO IS GET YOURSELF KILLED! YOU CAN'T SAVE HIM NOW! NOBODY CAN!

BLAM!

THERE'S TOO MANY OF THEM!!

WE'VE GOT TO GET OUT OF HERE!! WE'VE GOT TO LEAVE HIM!!

OH, GOD! WE CAN'T JUST--WE CAN'T!

IF WE'RE GOING TO GO--IT'S NOW OR NEVER!

COME ON!

WHAT DID WE DO, GLENN? WHAT DID WE JUST DO?

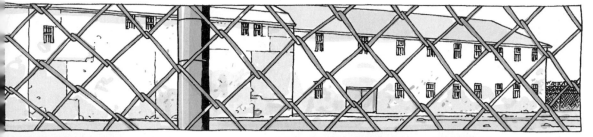

STILL WORRIED ABOUT RICK?

A *LITTLE*. I'M TRYING NOT TO *THINK* ABOUT IT, ACTUALLY.

SORRY.

SO IT WAS NICE OF DALE TO OFFER TO WATCH THE KIDS SO WE COULD CLEAN UP...

YEAH...

THIS IS *NICE* ISN'T IT? I STILL CAN'T GET OVER THE FACT THAT THIS PLACE STILL HAS *RUNNING WATER*.

I *SERIOUSLY* DOUBT THE WATER IS *TREATED* MUCH AT THIS POINT. IT'S STILL COMING TO US, BUT I DON'T THINK IT'S *CLEAN* ENOUGH TO DRINK WITHOUT BOILING.

UH-HUH.

IT DOESN'T *STINK*, THOUGH... SO I DON'T MIND SHOWERING IN--

AAAIIIEEEEK!!

I'M SORRY! I'M SORRY! I DIDN'T KNOW ANYONE WAS IN HERE! I SWEAR!

HEH. HEH.

AXEL, MAN--WHAT'S SO *FUNNY?* TELL ME, MAN.

WHERE'S *DEX* AT? YOU GUYS SHOULD GO TO THE SHOWER ROOM--GET YOU AN *EYE FULL*, YOU FOLLOW ME?

LORI AND CAROL ARE *BOTH* IN THERE, WET AND SOAPY. IT'S A MIGHTY *FINE* SIGHT.

DEXTER'S TAKING A *WALK*, OR SOMETHING. HE SAID HE NEEDED TO GET SOME *AIR*. 'SIDES, WE DON'T GO THAT WAY NO MORE.

NOT SINCE WE HOOKED UP, Y'KNOW.

YOU THINK THAT'S GONNA *KEEP*, ANDREW? NOW THAT WE'RE NOT *ALONE* IN HERE THAT IS. IF SO, YOU'RE SETTING YOURSELF UP FOR SOME *HEARTBREAK.*

OL' DEXTER'LL BE SWITCHING SIDES AS SOON AS HE FINDS HIM A WOMAN *WILLING* AND *ABLE*--YOU FOLLOW ME?

YOU BEST BE *READY* FOR THAT, OR YOU GET STUCK HOLDIN' YOUR *DICK.*

AIN'T *LIKE* THAT, MAN. YOU DON'T KNOW WHAT YOU'RE *TALKING* ABOUT.

WHATEVER. YOU'RE KIDDING YOURSELF AND YOU'RE MISSING A *HELLUVA* SHOW.

I GOTTA GET BACK TO MY *CELL* BEFORE I LOSE THIS *MENTAL IMAGE.*

MOM!

WERE YOU GOOD FOR UNCLE DALE?

YEAH, I JUST PLAYED WITH TOYS AND STUFF.

YOU SMELL REAL GOOD, MOM.

WHEN YOUR DAD GETS BACK, YOU'RE GOING TO HAVE TO TAKE A SHOWER TOO. THEN YOU'LL--

CARL, WHAT ARE YOU--?

I--

JESUS, GLENN-- WHAT HAPPENED?

OH, GOD! WHERE'S TYREESE?!

HE GOT AHEAD OF US--HE WAS-- *SURROUNDED.* THERE WERE SO MANY OF THEM AROUND HIM--THERE WAS *NOTHING* WE COULD *DO.* WE HAD TO--

WE HAD TO *LEAVE* HIM.

WHAT?

HE JUST--PLOWED INTO THEM--RAN INTO THE *CENTER* OF THE GYM. HE WAS *CRAZY*-- HE--

...

WHERE'S *MAGGIE?*

WHERE'S MY DAD?

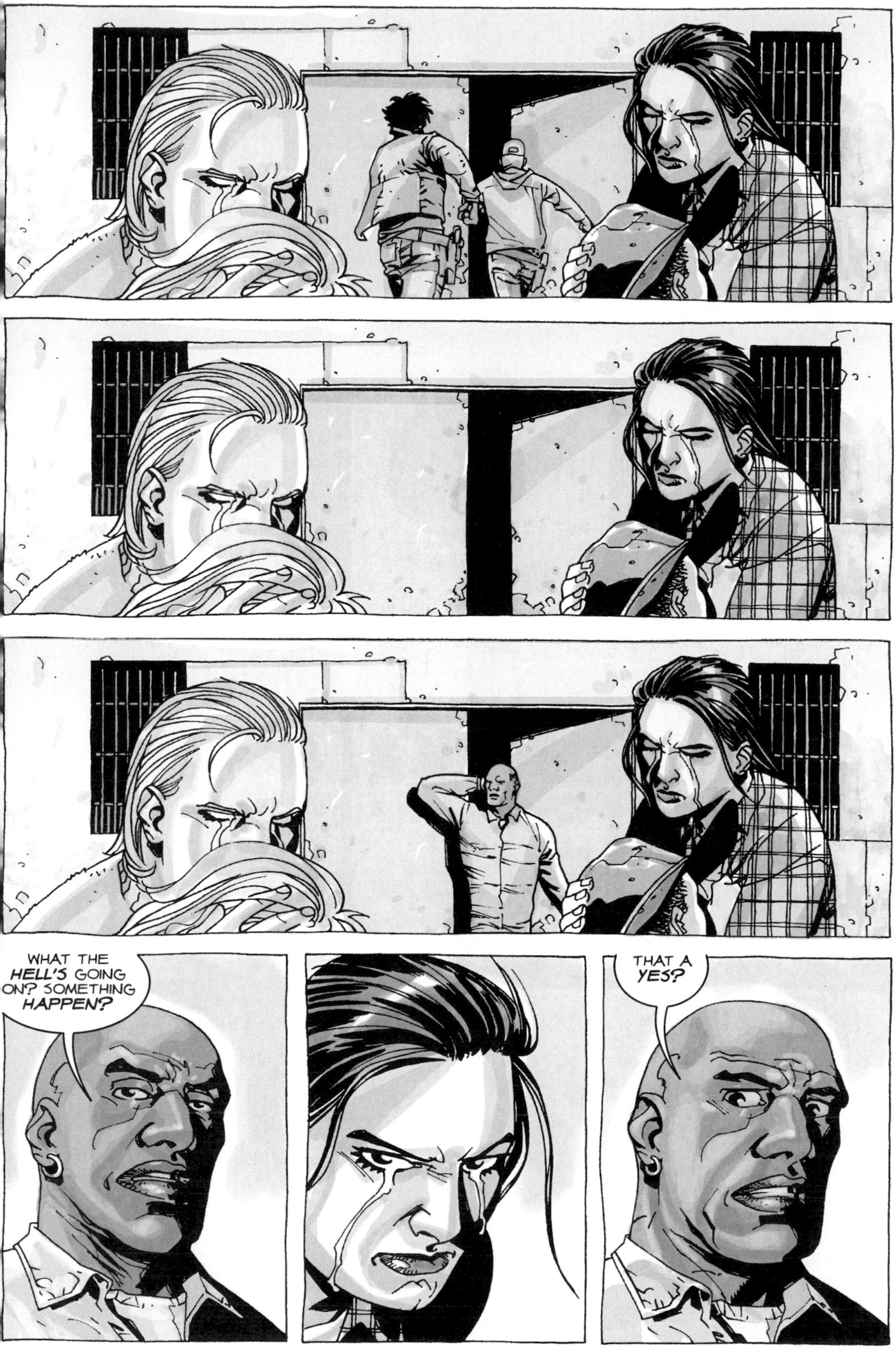
WHAT THE HELL'S GOING ON? SOMETHING HAPPEN?
THAT A YES?

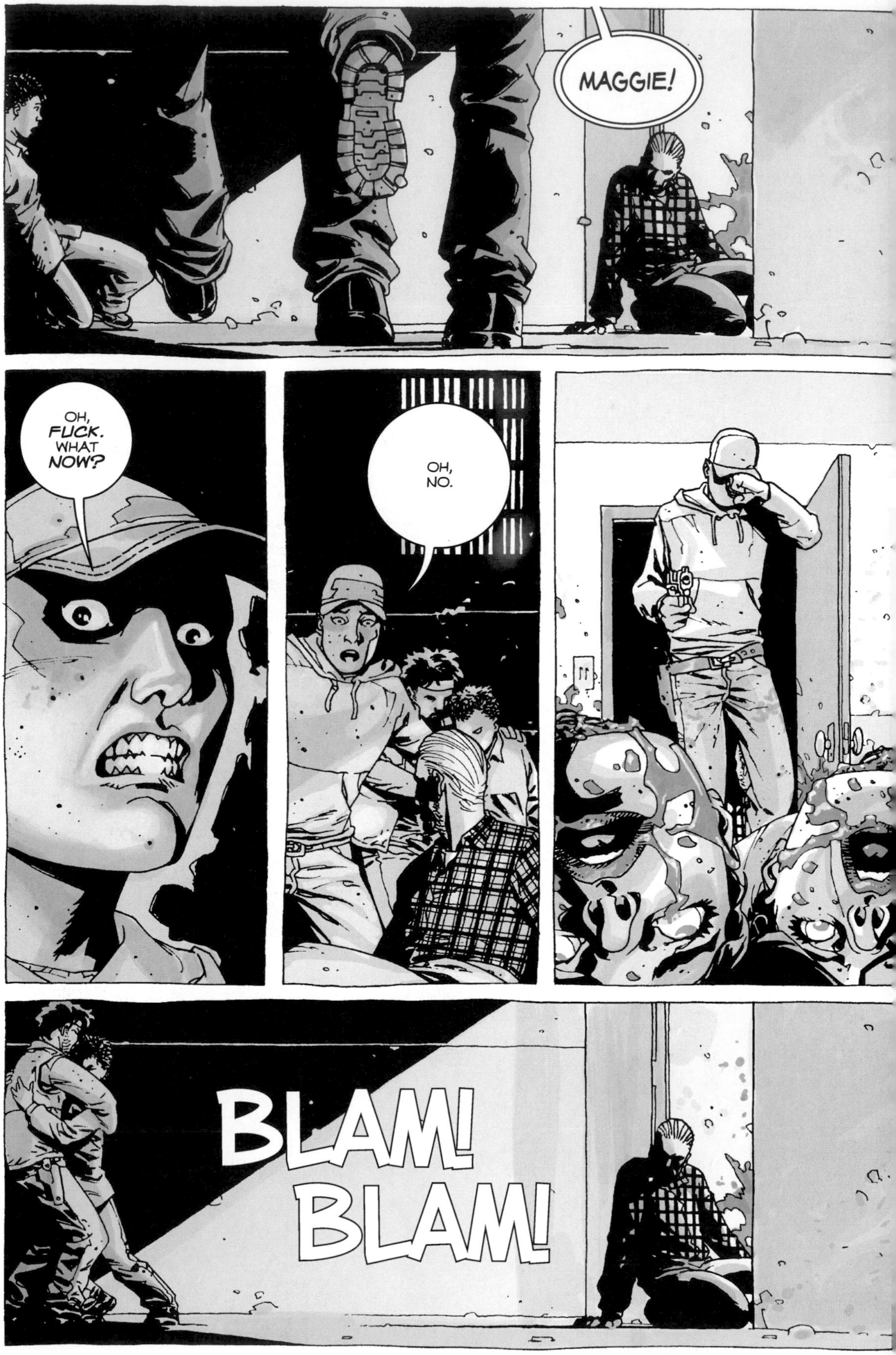
MAGGIE!
OH, FUCK. WHAT NOW?
OH, NO.
BLAM! BLAM!

YOU SICK FUCK!

DID YOU *KILL* THEM? *DID YOU KILL THEM,* YOU *MURDERER*?!

BEST GET OUT OF MY FACE BEFORE I--

DON'T YOU FUCKING *MOVE.*

GET UP!

WHAT'D WE *DO?* WE DIDN'T DO NOTHING!

JUST GO!

WHERE WERE YOU TODAY?! YOU'RE THE ONLY ONE WE *KNOW* IS CAPABLE OF THIS! UNTIL WE FIND OUT OTHERWISE-- YOU'RE NOT LEAVING THIS CELL.

MIND TELLING ME WHAT YOU THINK I *DID,* PSYCHO BITCH?

LIKE YOU DON'T KNOW.

CHRIST. I WAS GOING TO TAKE CARL'S GUN AWAY *TODAY*. I THOUGHT WE WERE *SAFE*. MAYBE IF RACHEL AND SUSIE HAD GUNS...

SOPHIA DOESN'T EVEN KNOW WHAT'S GOING ON. SHE'S--SHE'S SO *CONFUSED* BY ALL THIS *DEATH*, IT'S NOT EVEN REGISTERING THAT *TYREESE*--

OH, *GOD*.

THERE, THERE. JUST LET IT OUT. I'M *HERE* FOR YOU, *CAROL*. I'M HERE FOR YOU.

I *KNOW* YOU ARE. YOU'VE DONE *SO* MUCH TO HELP US LORI, YOU AND *RICK*...I DON'T KNOW HOW TO *THANK* YOU.

I OWE YOU SO MUCH...

I'M *SORRY*.

I'M *SO* SORRY.

IT'S OKAY...IT'S *OKAY*.

YOU'RE GOING THROUGH *A LOT* RIGHT NOW. DON'T EVEN *THINK* ABOUT IT.

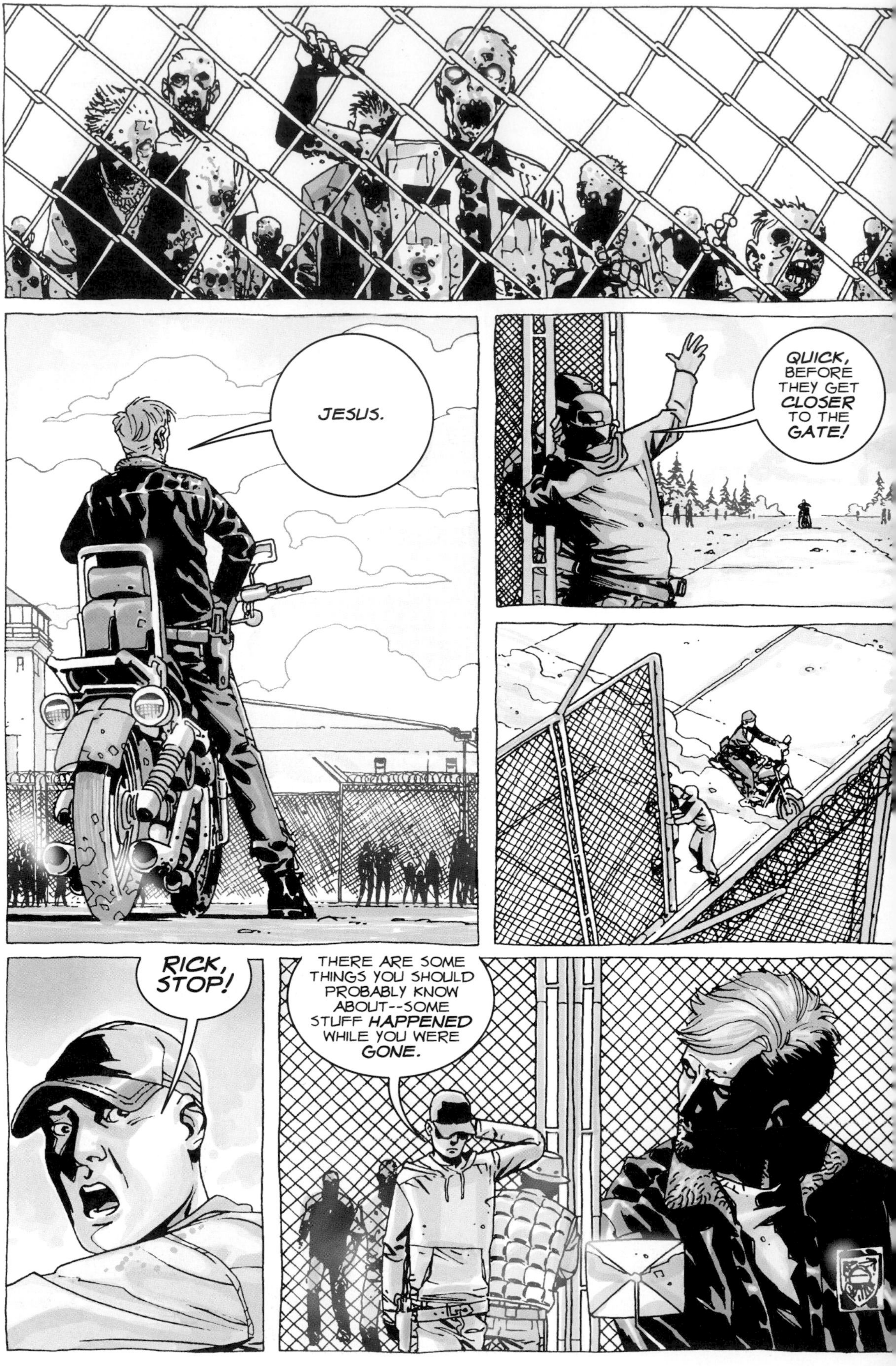
JESUS.
QUICK, BEFORE THEY GET CLOSER TO THE GATE!
RICK, STOP!
THERE ARE SOME THINGS YOU SHOULD PROBABLY KNOW ABOUT--SOME STUFF HAPPENED WHILE YOU WERE GONE.

WHAT HAPPENED? TELL ME!

HERSHEL'S GIRLS-- THE TWO *YOUNGEST*, NOT THE ONE GLENN'S WITH, WERE KILLED. IT *HAD* TO BE SOMEONE IN THE PRISON. WE THINK IT WAS *DEXTER*, THE BIG BLACK FELLA. WE LOCKED HIM UP.

DEAD? OH, *LORD*.

I TOLD THEM IT WAS *SAFE* HERE-- THIS IS *MY* FAULT.

TYREESE--HE WANTED TO CLEAN ALL THE *DEAD* OUT OF THE *GYM*. ONCE WE GOT IN THERE--HE WENT *CRAZY*. HE RAN OUT INTO THE MIDDLE OF THEM, GOT *SURROUNDED*.

WE COULDN'T SAVE HIM--WE HAD TO *LEAVE* HIM. HE'S STILL IN THERE...THERE WAS NOTHING *ELSE* WE COULD *DO*.

HE'S *DEAD*? DID YOU *SEE* HIS *BODY*?

HE WAS SURROUNDED-- THERE WAS *NOTHING* WE COULD *DO*.

WE HAVEN'T HEARD *ANY* GUN SHOTS SINCE HE WAS LEFT IN THERE--HE DIDN'T MAKE IT.

FOR *GOD'S SAKE*, ANSWER ME!

DID YOU SEE HIS *BODY*?! ARE YOU *SURE* HE WAS KILLED?!

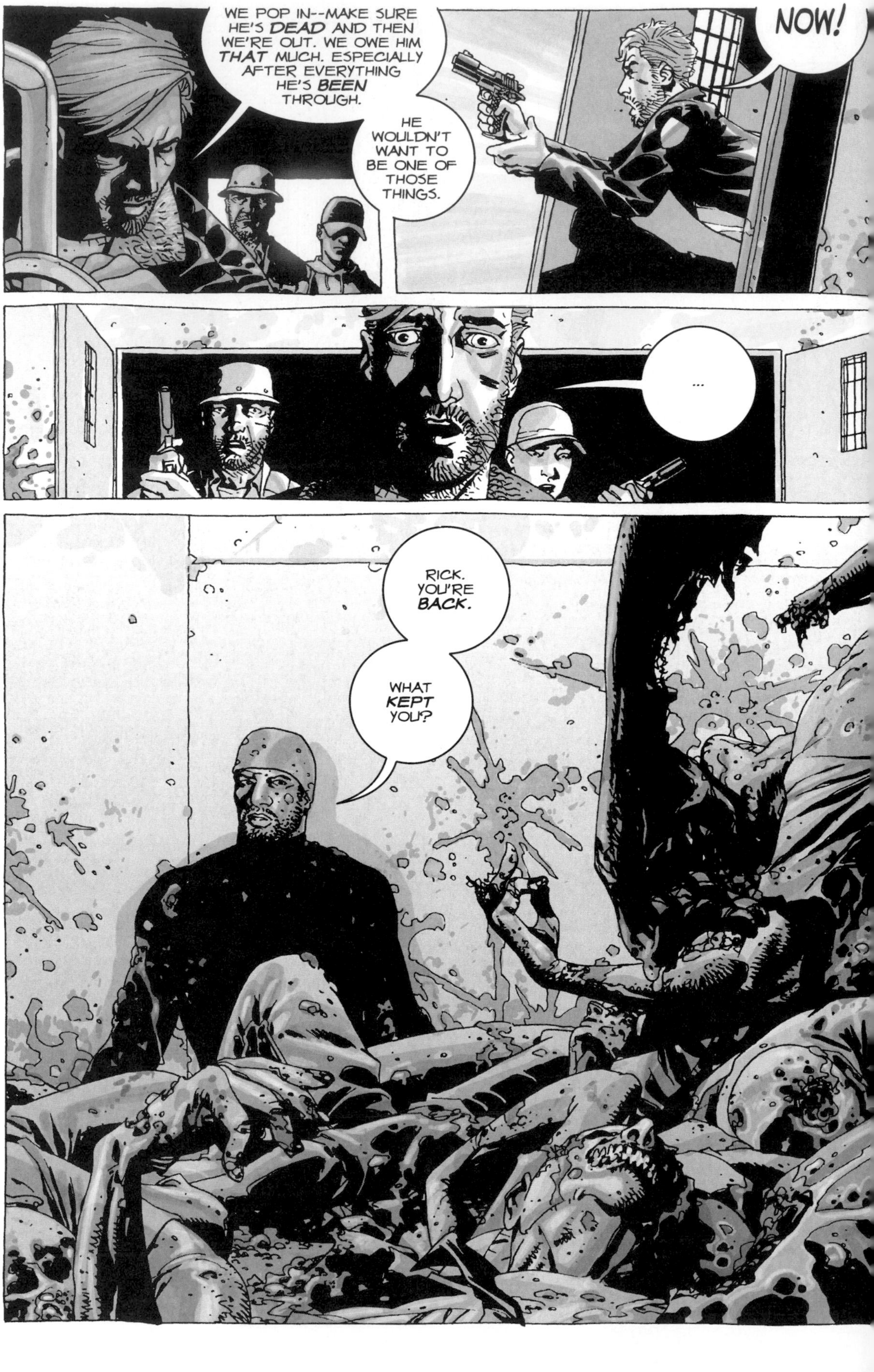

WE POP IN--MAKE SURE HE'S DEAD AND THEN WE'RE OUT. WE OWE HIM THAT MUCH. ESPECIALLY AFTER EVERYTHING HE'S BEEN THROUGH.
HE WOULDN'T WANT TO BE ONE OF THOSE THINGS.
NOW!
...
RICK. YOU'RE BACK.
WHAT KEPT YOU?

YOU CAME BACK.

I DID, YEAH.

DAD!!

TYREESE! OH MY GOD!!

CAREFUL--I AIN'T SHOWERED. I HAD SO MUCH *MUCK* ON ME, WE'RE GOING TO HAVE TO *BURN* MY CLOTHES.

I DON'T CARE. HOLD ME.

SO HE WAS--?

ALIVE-- JUST *SITTING* IN THERE. I HAVE *NO IDEA* HOW. IT'S A *GODDAMN MIRACLE.*

GONNA TELL ME WHERE YOU *WENT?*

YEAH. I'LL TELL YOU *ALL* ABOUT IT, BUT NOT RIGHT NOW. RIGHT NOW THERE'S SOMETHING *ELSE* I'VE GOT TO DO.

DID YOU DO IT?

FUCK NO, I DIDN'T "DO IT." YOUR PSYCHO KNOCKED-UP WIFE LOCKED ME IN HERE BECAUSE I'D DONE MY WIFE AN' HER BOYFRIEND. THING IS, I AIN'T KILLING NO ONE ELSE. HAD MY FILL OF IT, Y'KNOW?

YOU LOOKING FOR SUSPECTS LOOK IN THAT PACK OF FREAKS YOU HANG WITH. MY CREW WAS LOCKED IN THAT CAFETERIA FOR MONTHS AND WE DIDN'T KILL EACH OTHER. I THINK ONE OF YOUR PEOPLE'S SNAPPED.

LUCKILY-- I'M SAFE AS CAN BE IN HERE.

IF I FIND OUT YOU DID IT, I'LL BEAT YOU TO DEATH MYSELF.

YOU CAN'T TALK TO ME LIKE THAT. COME ON THE OTHER SIDE A' THEM BARS, COUNTRY BOY.

I DARE YOU.

YOU'RE ALL FUCKING CRAZY--EVERY LAST ONE OF YOU.

LOCK THAT DAMN DOOR ON YOUR WAY OUT.

MORNING, ANDREA. WHAT ARE YOU UP TO?

OH, HEY. I'M JUST GATHERING UP SOME OF THE *CLOTHES* THAT WERE LEFT IN THESE DRYERS.

WITH EVERYONE RUNNING OUT OF THINGS TO WEAR, I FIGURE THESE PRISON UNIFORMS WILL COME IN HANDY.

IF I HURRY I'LL BE ABLE TO GET THESE TO *LORI* IN TIME FOR THE MORNING WASH. WE COULD ALL HAVE A CHANGE OF CLOTHES BY MIDDAY.

DO YOU WANT TO *HELP*?

NOT PARTICULARLY, *NO.*

WELL, THOMAS... IF YOU'RE NOT GOING TO *HELP,* WHY'D YOU COME DOWN HERE?

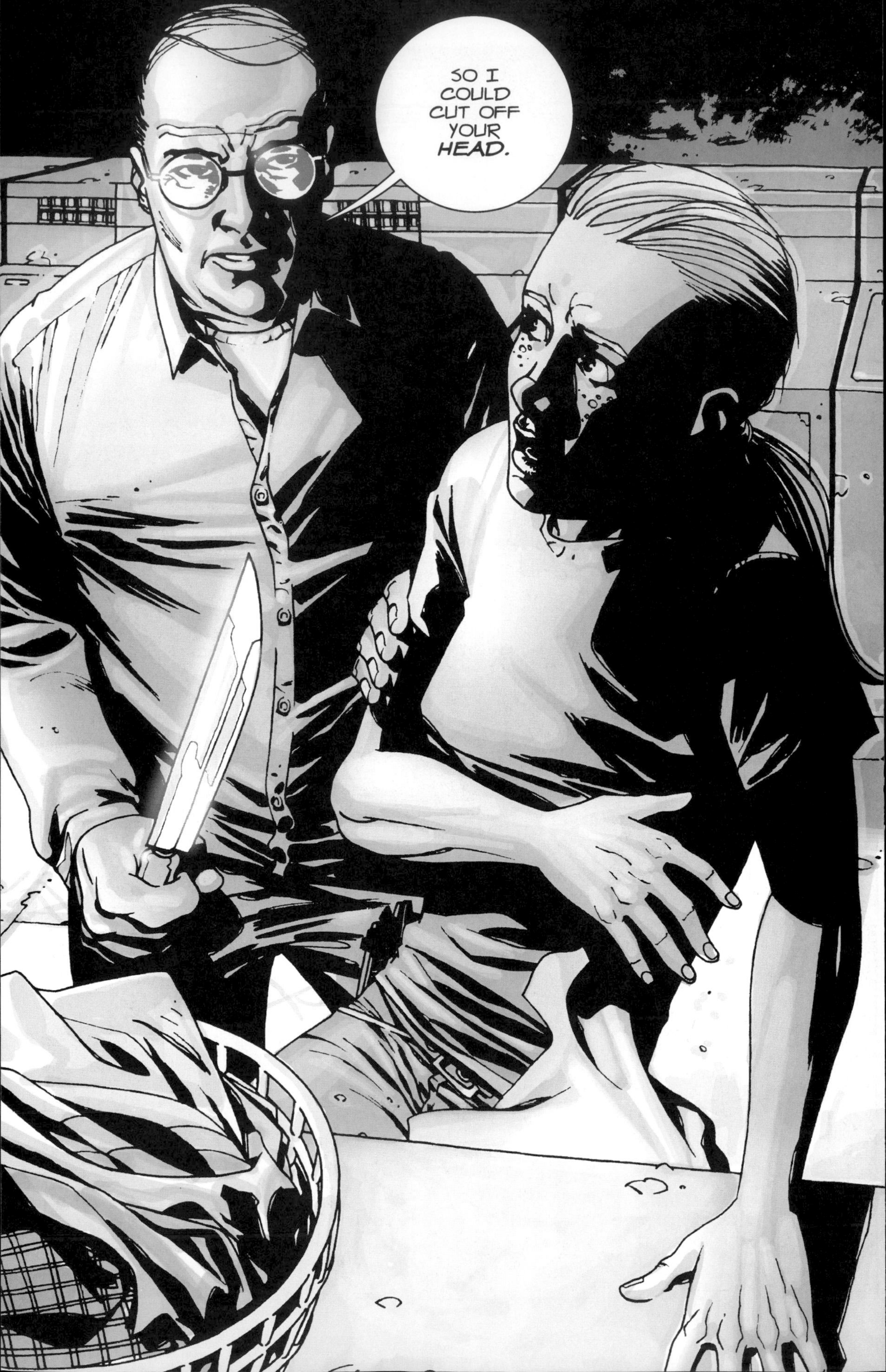
SO I COULD CUT OFF YOUR HEAD.

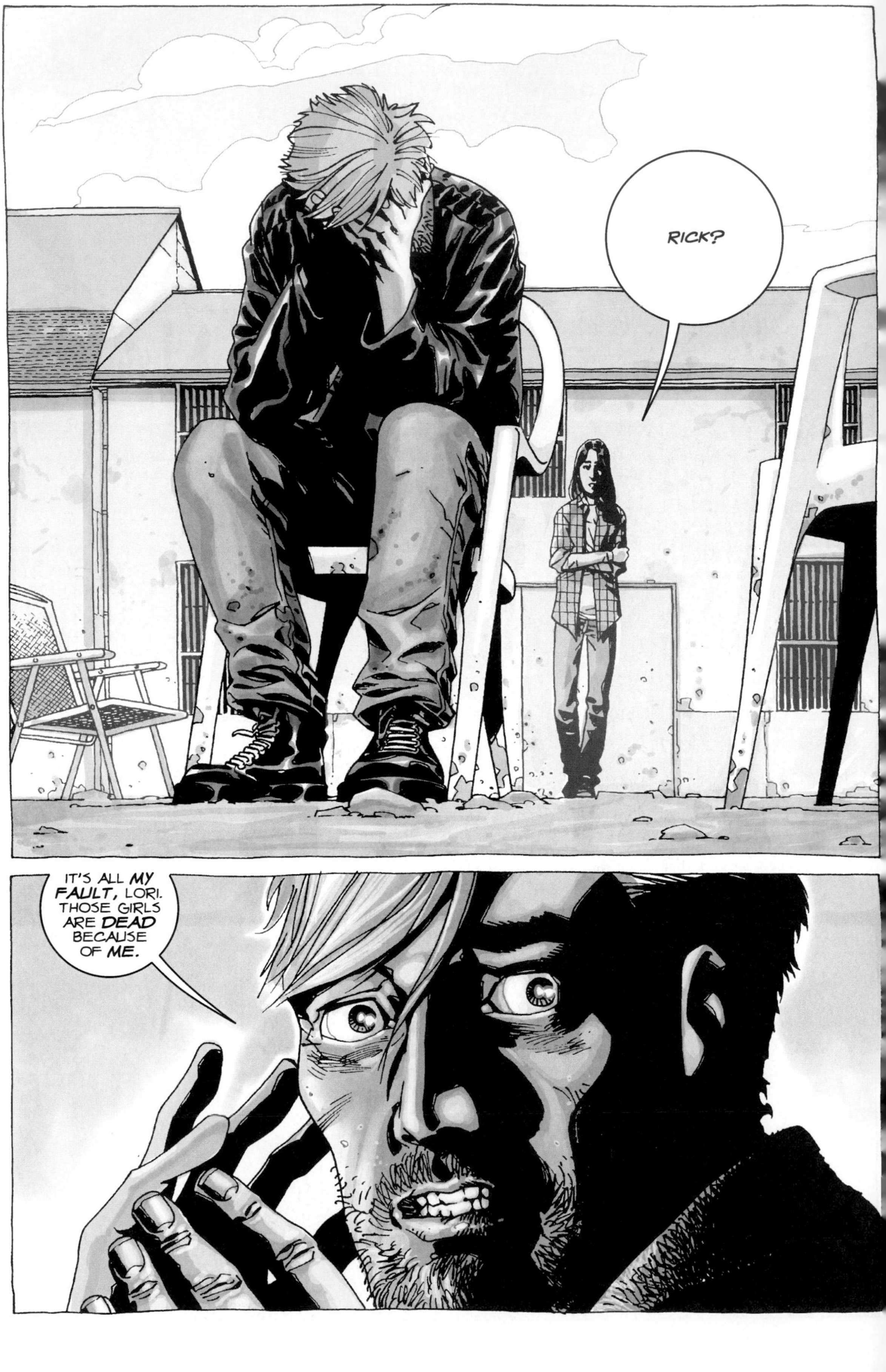
RICK?
IT'S ALL MY FAULT, LORI. THOSE GIRLS ARE DEAD BECAUSE OF ME.

I THOUGHT THIS PLACE WAS *SAFE.* I *TOLD* HERSHEL IT WOULD BE *SAFE* HERE. I *ASSURED* HIM. I TALKED HIM *INTO* COMING HERE.

IF HE HAD KEPT THEM ON HIS FARM, THEY'D STILL BE *ALIVE.* IF IT WASN'T FOR *ME*--WANTING TO *HELP* THEM, THEY'D BE *OKAY.*

HERSHEL HAS LOST *SO MUCH*--MORE THAN *ANY* OF US. HE TRUSTED ME... HE *BELIEVED* ME...I LET HIM *DOWN.* I DON'T KNOW WHAT TO *DO* LORI.

I *KILLED* HIS *DAUGHTERS.*

RICK, THAT'S *BULLSHIT!* YOU WERE OUT THERE-- YOU *SAW* ALL THE DEAD THAT ARE ROAMING AROUND NOW THAT IT'S *WARM.* WE HAVEN'T HEARD FROM OTIS IN *DAYS.* WE DON'T KNOW *WHAT'S* GOING ON OUT THERE!

WE JUST DON'T HAVE *TIME* FOR THIS.

YOU HAVE NO WAY OF KNOWING *WHAT* WOULD HAVE HAPPENED. SO STOP BLAMING YOURSELF.

I'M *SORRY,* LORI. I'M--I'M NOT ALL *HERE.* I HAVEN'T BEEN ABLE TO *SLEEP* SINCE JULIE AND CHRIS--I CAN *BARELY* THINK STRAIGHT.

I *KNOW,* RICK. I'VE *SEEN* YOU. YOU NEED TO *REST.*

WHAT DID YOU *DO* YESTERDAY? WHERE DID YOU *GO?*

I WENT BACK TO *THE CAMP.* I DUG UP SHANE.

AND I SHOT HIM.

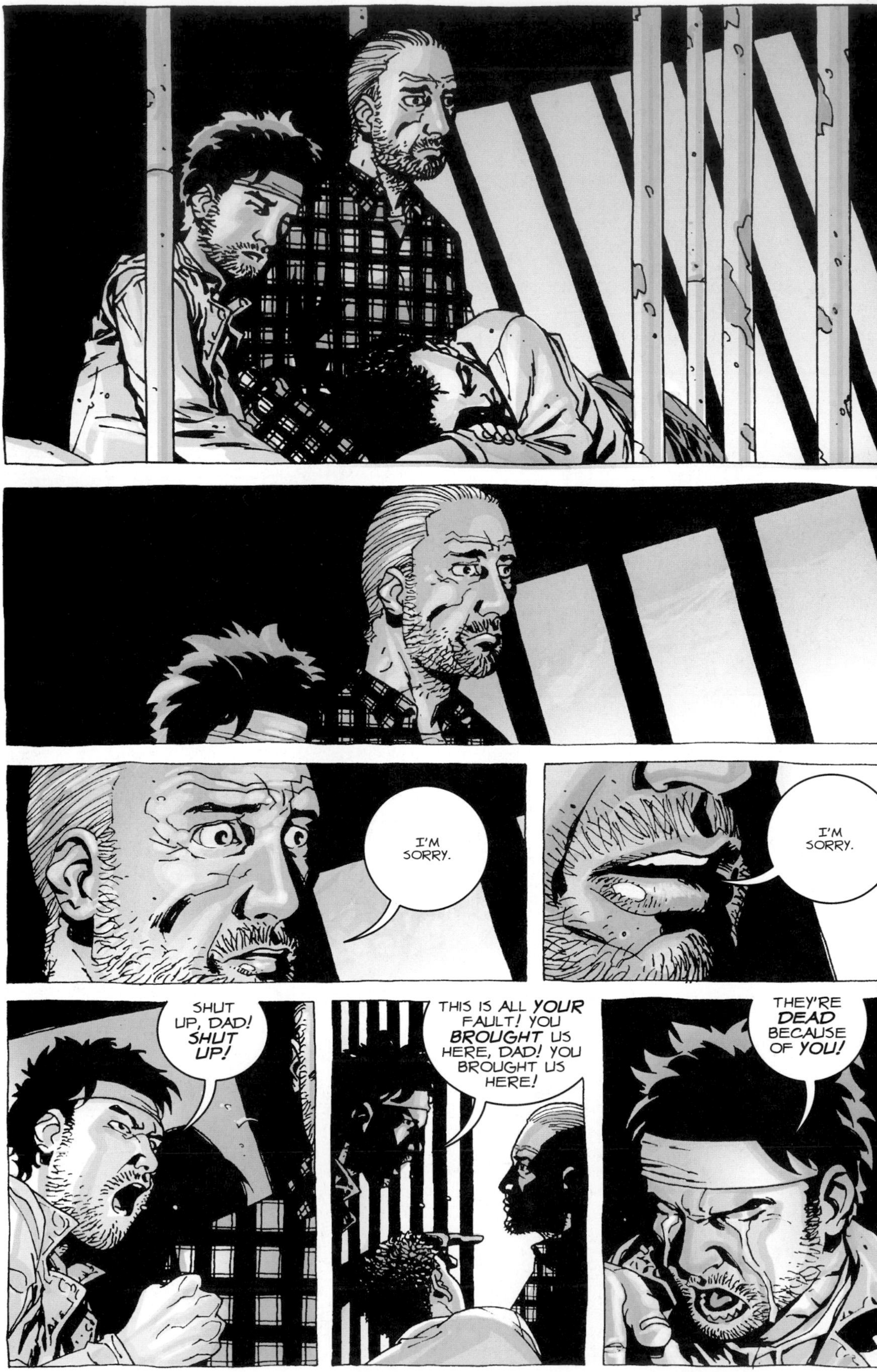
I'M SORRY.
I'M SORRY.
SHUT UP, DAD! **SHUT UP!**
THIS IS ALL **YOUR** FAULT! YOU **BROUGHT** US HERE, DAD! YOU BROUGHT US HERE!
THEY'RE **DEAD** BECAUSE OF **YOU!**

=PSST!=

DEX!

HEY, MAN--YOU *OKAY* IN THERE?

I'M IN *HERE*--I'M NOT *OKAY*. GET IT?

FEEL LIKE A FUCKING *PRISONER* AGAIN.

YOU THINK OF *ANYTHING* I CAN DO, MAN-- *ANYTHING* AT *ALL* TO GET YOU OUTTA THERE, AND I'LL *DO IT*. I DON'T CARE *WHAT* IT IS.

JUST SAY THE WORD, MAN. JUST SAY *THE WORD.*

IF YOU *SERIOUS,* LITTLE MAN--YOU LISTEN UP. THESE *FUCKS* AIN'T OUR *FRIENDS.* THEY AIN'T FUCKING *NORMAL.* THEY *CRAZIES.* THEY THOUGHT *WE* WAS LIVING THE *HIGH LIFE* IN THAT CAFETERIA. WHAT THEY BEEN THROUGH, OUT IN THE *WORLD*-- IT'S TORE 'EM UP. THEY *BROKEN.*

NOW THEY KILLING EACH OTHER AN' BLAMIN' *US.* ONLY *ONE WAY* OUT OF THIS.

YOU GOTTA FIGURE OUT A WAY INTO *A BLOCK*--WHERE THE GUARD CENTER IS. THAT'S WHERE THEY GOT THE *RIOT GEAR* AND THE *SHOTGUNS* AN' SHIT. ENOUGH AMMO TO KILL AN *ARMY* IN THERE. THEY STOCKED UP FOR *RIOTS.* YOU GET IN THERE, WE *HOME FREE.*

YOU JUST GOTTA DO IT ON THE *DOWN LOW.* I *NEVER* TRUSTED THESE FUCKS-- *THEY* DON'T KNOW ABOUT THE GUNS.

UNDER- STAND?

I GET *THOSE*-- AND WE CAN BUST YOU OUTTA HERE IN A *BLAZE OF GLORY.* KICKING ALL *KINDS* OF ASS!

THAT'S WHAT'S *GOTTA* HAPPEN. OTHERWISE I *ROT* IN HERE UNTIL THEY DECIDE TO *OFF* ME. AND IT'S *YOU* NEXT.

THINK YOU CAN GET IN THERE?

BROTHER, I CAN *FIND* A WAY.

OKAY--IF THESE THINGS KEEP PILING UP AGAINST THE FENCE, IT'S NOT IMPOSSIBLE FOR THE SHEER *WEIGHT* OF THEIR NUMBERS TO PUSH THE FENCE OVER. WE COULD EVENTUALLY HAVE *THOUSANDS* OUT HERE.

EVENTUALLY.

SINCE WE'RE LOW ON *BULLETS*, WE CAN'T JUST *SHOOT* THEM... SO *HOPEFULLY* THIS WILL *WORK*.

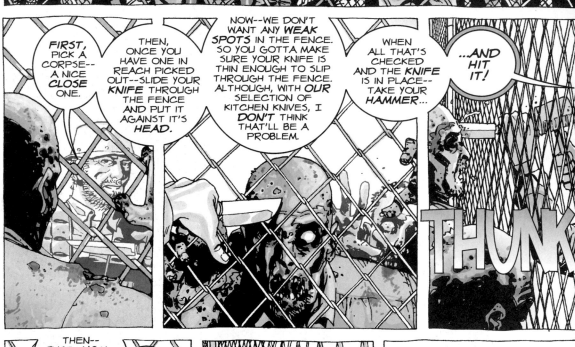

FIRST, PICK A *CORPSE*-- A NICE *CLOSE* ONE.

THEN, ONCE YOU HAVE ONE IN REACH PICKED OUT--SLIDE YOUR *KNIFE* THROUGH THE FENCE AND PUT IT AGAINST IT'S *HEAD*.

NOW--WE DON'T WANT ANY *WEAK SPOTS* IN THE FENCE. SO YOU GOTTA MAKE SURE YOUR KNIFE IS THIN ENOUGH TO SLIP THROUGH THE FENCE. ALTHOUGH, WITH *OUR* SELECTION OF KITCHEN KNIVES, I *DON'T* THINK THAT'LL BE A PROBLEM.

WHEN ALL THAT'S CHECKED AND THE *KNIFE* IS IN PLACE-- TAKE YOUR *HAMMER*...

...AND HIT IT!

THUNK

THEN-- JUST--*UGH*-- PULL THE *KNIFE*--

OUT!

AUAAGH!

WHUMP!

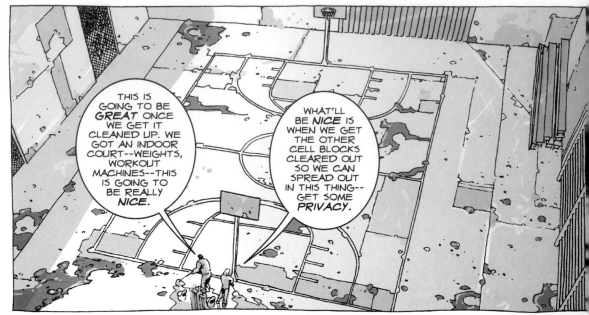

THIS IS GOING TO BE *GREAT* ONCE WE GET IT CLEANED UP. WE GOT AN INDOOR COURT--WEIGHTS, WORKOUT MACHINES--THIS IS GOING TO BE REALLY *NICE.*

WHAT'LL BE *NICE* IS WHEN WE GET THE OTHER CELL BLOCKS CLEARED OUT SO WE CAN SPREAD OUT IN THIS THING-- GET SOME *PRIVACY.*

I'M HEARING YOU ON *THAT* FRONT, CAROL-- I'M ABOUT *DUE* FOR SOME *ALONE* TIME.

REALLY, TYREESE? IS THAT *SO?* ALLEN IS WATCHING SOPHIA--AND THERE'S A *CLEAN* SPOT ON THE *FLOOR* BACK THERE--LOOKS *REALLY* COMFY.

WHO AM I TO DENY A WOMAN WHAT SHE *WANTS?*

JUST BE *QUICK* ABOUT IT--THIS FLOOR IS *COLD.*

YOU BE QUICK. *I'M* GOING TO TAKE MY *TIME.*

YES, SIR.

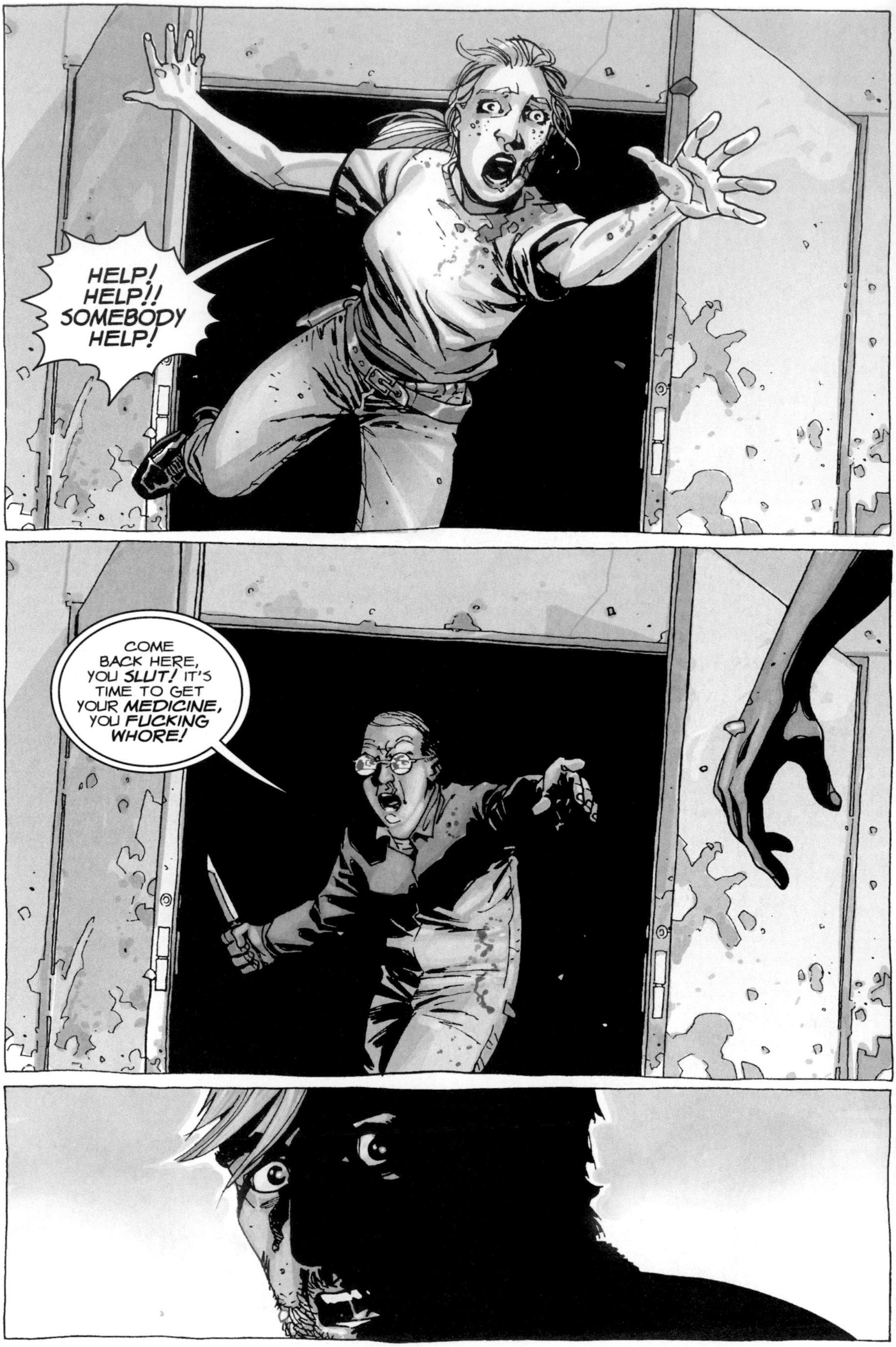
HELP! HELP!! SOMEBODY HELP!
COME BACK HERE, YOU SLUT! IT'S TIME TO GET YOUR MEDICINE, YOU FUCKING WHORE!

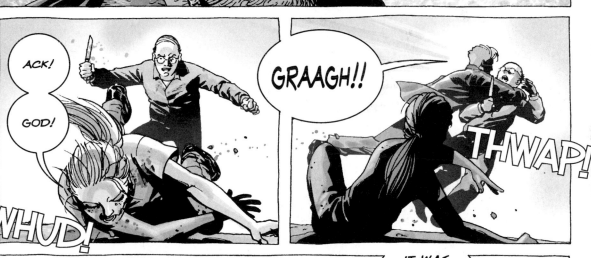

DON'T STOP HIM!

HE DESERVES *EVERY BIT* OF THIS, LORI.

WRAMM!

DON'T YOU?! YOU PSYCHO SON OF A BITCH!

DON'T YOU DESERVE THIS?!

RICK-- JESUS, MAN?! WHAT ARE YOU DOING?

HE *KILLED* THEM, TYREESE. HE *KILLED* A COUPLE OF *HELPLESS* LITTLE GIRLS!

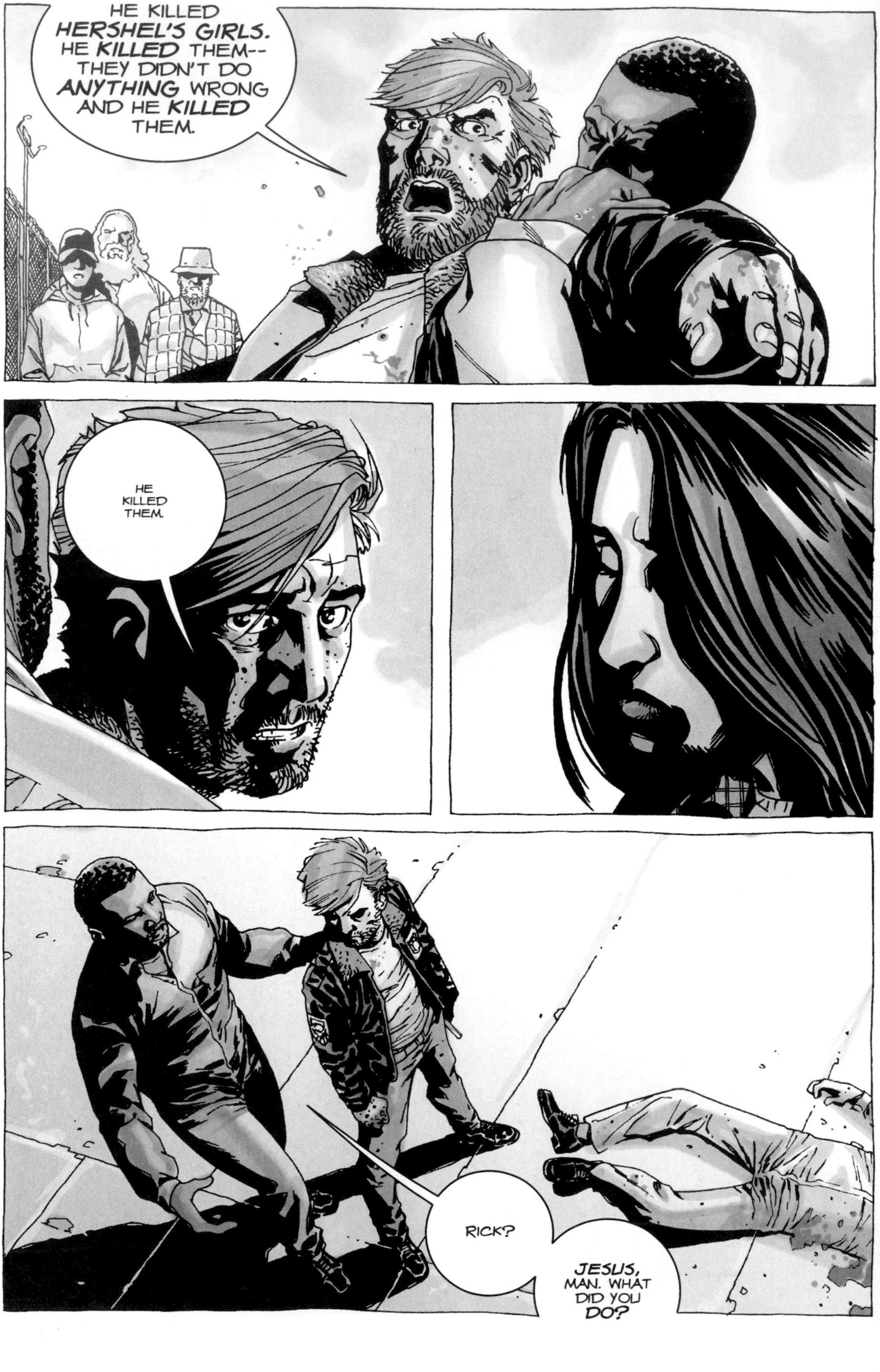
HE KILLED HERSHEL'S GIRLS. HE KILLED THEM-- THEY DIDN'T DO ANYTHING WRONG AND HE KILLED THEM.
HE KILLED THEM.
RICK?
JESUS, MAN. WHAT DID YOU DO?

HE KILLED THEM.

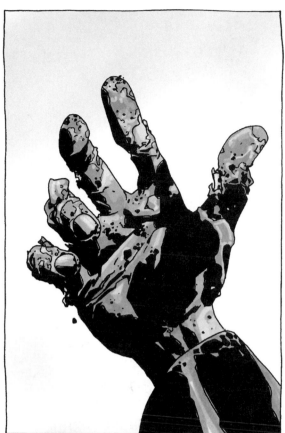

HE KILLED HERSHEL'S GIRLS.

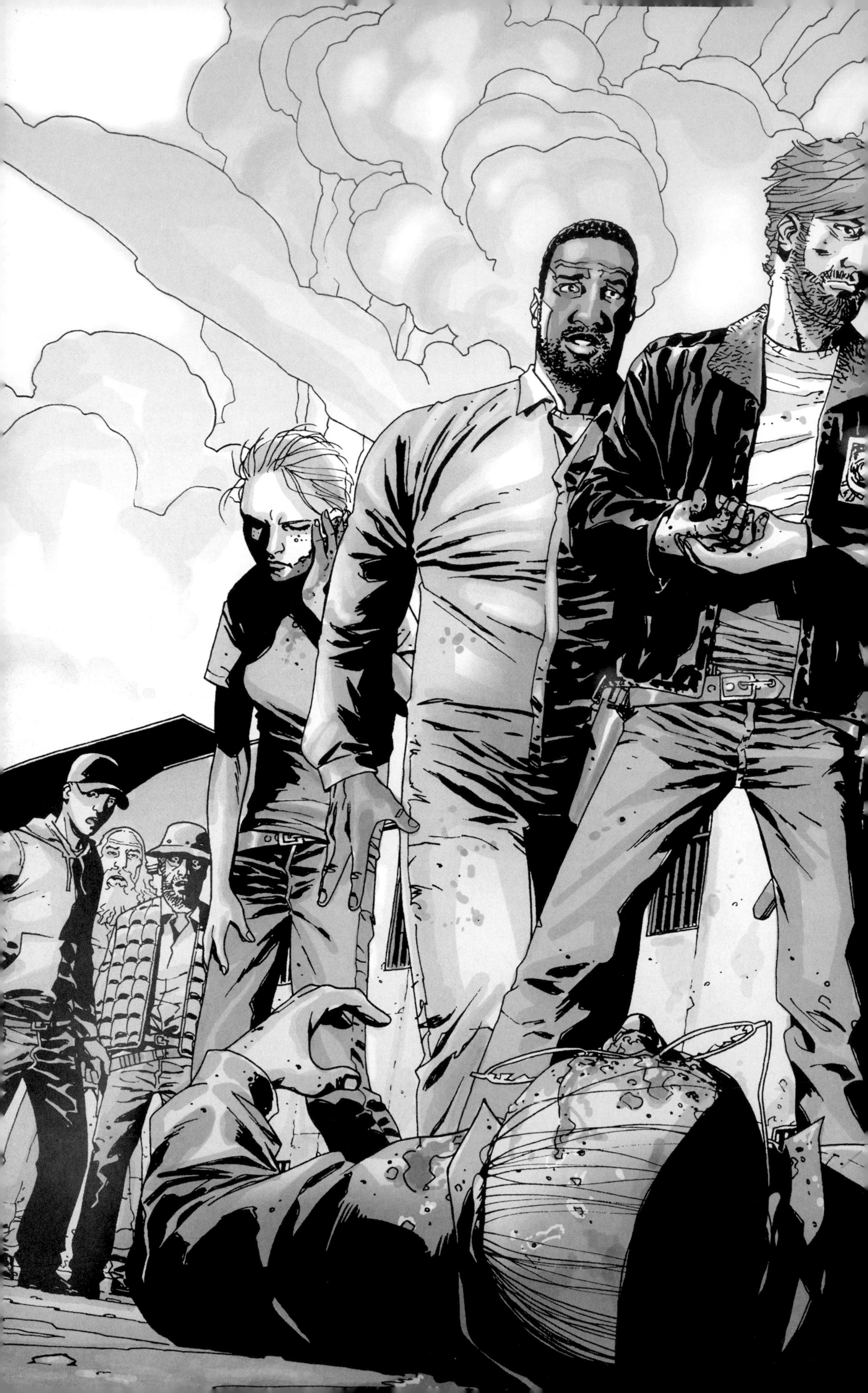

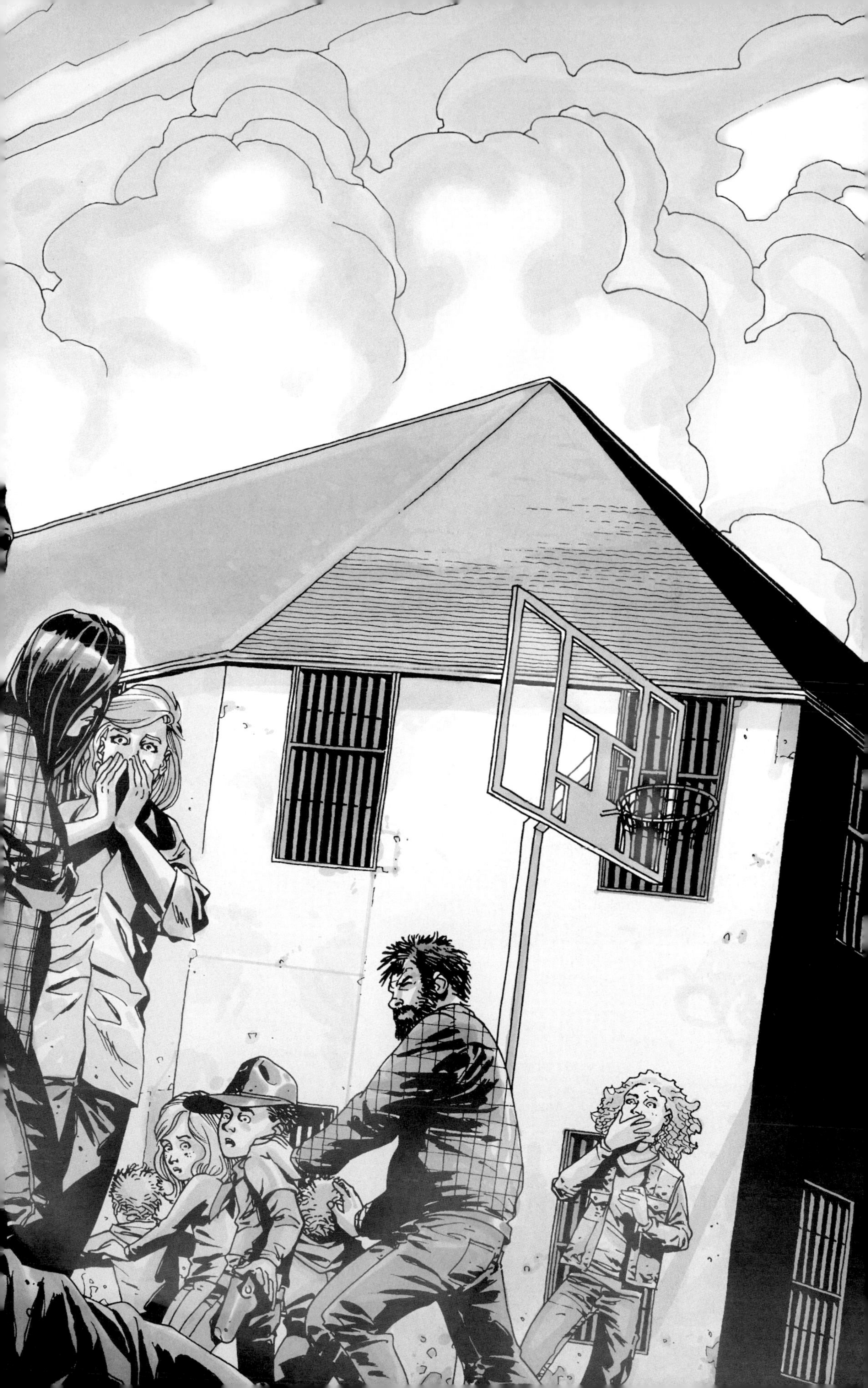

IS HE *DEAD?*

NO. NOT *YET.*

WHAT DO YOU MEAN BY *THAT?!* WHAT ARE YOU PLANNING ON *DOING,* RICK?

WHAT WOULD YOU HAVE ME *DO,* LORI?! *JUST LET HIM GO?!* HOPE THAT THE *NEXT* TIME HE *KILLS* IT'S SOMEONE WE HAVEN'T *MET?* IS THAT WHAT YOU *WANT?*

WE HAVE TO DO WHAT'S *RIGHT*--TO MAKE SURE HE NEVER KILLS *AGAIN!*

I SEEM TO RECALL HEARING ABOUT YOU BEING PRETTY GODDAMN *ANGRY* WITH *DEXTER* WHEN YOU THOUGHT *HE* WAS THE ONE--THAT ALL IT TAKES? A *DAY* SO THAT YOU CAN FORGET THE CRIME? YOU NOT TOO *CONCERNED* WITH THIS NOW?

SO THAT'S HOW THINGS *ARE?!* YOU *SAY* WHAT WE'RE GOING TO *DO* AND WE *DO* IT? YOU'RE THE *KING* NOW?

WE'VE GOT A CHANCE TO *CHANGE* THINGS, RICK. WE'VE GOT A CHANCE TO BREAK THE CYCLE. *NO KILLING* MEANS *NO KILLING.* IF WE KILL HIM--WE'RE NO BETTER THAN *HE* IS.

LETTING HIM LOOSE OUT THERE ON HIS OWN IS ALMOST A *WORSE* PUNISHMENT--AT LEAST *THEN* WE WOULDN'T HAVE ANY *BLOOD* ON OUR HANDS!

OR WE COULD JUST LOCK HIM UP *HERE!*

NO WAY! NO *FUCKING* WAY!

I'M *NOT* GOING TO SLEEP HERE AT NIGHT KNOWING HE COULD GET OUT--AND *ATTACK* ME AGAIN!

AND WE'RE *NOT* THROWING HIM TO THE ZOMBIES UNLESS I CAN *WATCH* THEM *TEAR* HIS ASS *APART!* LOOK WHAT THAT *FUCK DID* TO ME!

HE DESERVES TO *DIE* FOR WHAT HE DID TO THOSE GIRLS!

WE HAVEN'T MADE *ANY* KINDS OF *RULES* FOR THIS SORT OF *THING.* IF WE'RE GOING TO START A *NEW LIFE* HERE--TRY TO REESTABLISH *SOCIETY*--WE NEED TO HAVE *RULES* FOR THIS.

WE NEED TO ALL DECIDE WHAT WE *DO.*

WHAT DO WE *DO?*

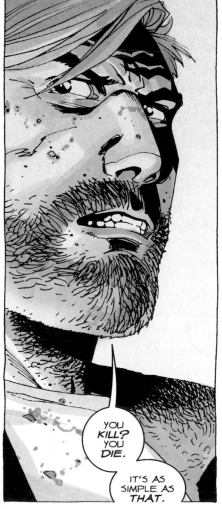

YOU *KILL?* YOU *DIE.*

IT'S AS SIMPLE AS *THAT.*

THAT WORKS FOR *ME*.

HE WAS *SO*... HE WAS...

NICE.

SO THAT'S *IT*? YOU'RE JUST MAKING THE DECISION FOR *ALL OF US* THEN?!

I'M JUST MAKING SURE WE DO WHAT'S *RIGHT*, LORI. I WAS PUT IN CHARGE AFTER WE LEFT ATLANTA.

HONEY, *LISTEN* TO ME. I'M A *COP*--I'VE BEEN *TRAINED* TO MAKE DECISIONS LIKE THIS. I'M THE *ONLY* ONE HERE IN A POSITION OF *AUTHORITY*.

I'M MAKING THE *CHOICE* THAT'S *BEST* FOR *ALL* OF US. THAT'S WHAT YOU ALL *LOOK UP* TO ME FOR. THAT'S WHY *EVERYONE* COMES TO ME FOR *ADVICE* AND *GUIDANCE*.

I'M IN CHARGE.

LISTEN TO *YOURSELF*. YOU'RE MY *HUSBAND*, YOU PRICK--NOT MY *FATHER*!

LORI-- SHUT THE *FUCK* UP.

THANKS FOR GETTING THE KIDS OUT OF THERE, *ALLEN.*

CARL!

ARE YOU OKAY, SON?

IS DAD *CRAZY?*

IS HE GOING TO *KILL* US?!

NO, CARL-- *NO!* COME HERE.

HE JUST *ATTACKED* THAT MAN. HE WOULDN'T STOP *HITTING* HIM, MOM. WHY DID HE HIT HIM *SO MUCH?*

YOUR DAD HAD A *REASON* TO ATTACK THAT MAN. HE KILLED RACHEL AND SUSIE-- *TRIED* TO KILL *ANDREA.* HE WAS A *BAD MAN.*

BAD LIKE *SHANE?*

YEAH--*A LOT* LIKE SHANE.

ONLY I KILLED SHANE *BEFORE* HE KILLED ANYBODY.

THAT'S RIGHT, BUT-- BUT YOU-- DID THE *RIGHT* THING.

SO DID I.

ALLEN, COULD YOU GIVE US A *MINUTE*?

SURE THING, RICK. C'MON KIDS, LET'S GIVE THE *GRIMES* FAMILY SOME TIME TO *TALK.*

I'M NOT MAKING THESE DECISIONS *LIGHTLY*, LORI. I'M THINKING EVERYTHING THROUGH.

I KNOW THINGS GOT A LITTLE *HEATED* OUTSIDE EARLIER AND I MAY NOT HAVE SEEMED COMPLETELY *RATIONAL*-- BUT I WAS.

I'M AN OFFICER OF THE *LAW.* I MAY NOT HAVE ANYONE TO *ANSWER* TO ANYMORE-- BUT THESE PEOPLE LOOK TO ME TO KEEP THEM *SAFE.* I *OWE* IT TO THEM TO DO EVERYTHING IN MY POWER TO DO SO.

WHERE I SEE *JUSTICE,* YOU SEE ANOTHER *MURDER.* MORE THAN ANYONE ELSE OUT HERE--I NEED *YOU* ON MY SIDE, HON'. I JUST CAN'T *LIVE* WITH IT OTHERWISE. I NEED YOU TO SEE *MY* SIDE OF THINGS.

I DON'T KNOW *WHAT* I SEE ANYMORE, RICK.

OKAY--YOU SIT RIGHT THERE. I STILL HAVE THE *FIRST AID* KIT FROM THE *RV*. LET ME GET IT.

HERSHEL'D PROBABLY DO A BETTER JOB PATCHING YOU UP BUT I DON'T THINK HE'S *READY* TO HELP *ANYONE* AFTER WHAT HE JUST WENT THROUGH.

I'M NOT IN TOO GOOD A MOOD *EITHER*--THAT FUCKER *DID* JUST TRY TO *KILL* ME.

JESUS! THIS *FUCKING* HURTS!

LOOK FORWARD--LET ME MAKE SURE I CAN STOP THIS BLEEDING. I THINK MOST OF IT'S *STOPPED* ALREADY. THIS'LL BE *MOSTLY* CLEAN UP.

DID HE CUT MY *EAR?* TELL ME HE DIDN'T CUT MY EAR. IT *FELT* LIKE HE DID, BUT I NEVER HAD A CHANCE TO CHECK.

YOUR LOBE IS *GONE*--BUT YOU'LL STILL BE ABLE TO *HEAR.*

I COULDN'T CARE *LESS* ABOUT HEARING. I DON'T WANT TO LOOK LIKE A *FREAK.*

YOU'VE GOT NOTHING TO WORRY ABOUT. YOU'LL BE AS PRETTY AS *EVER*, AS SOON AS WE CLEAN YOU UP.

GOT ANYTHING *LEFT* IN THAT FIRST AID KIT THAT I COULD USE?

I'VE GOT OVER HALF A BOTTLE OF *PEROXIDE* HERE WITH YOUR *NAME* ON IT. HAVE A SEAT AND LET'S LOOK AT THAT *HAND*.

LET ME *WARN* YOU--IT'S *NOT* PRETTY.

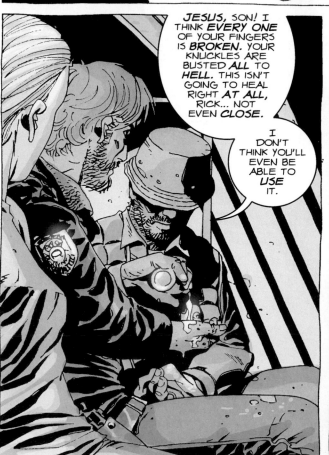

JESUS, SON! I THINK *EVERY ONE* OF YOUR FINGERS IS *BROKEN*. YOUR KNUCKLES ARE BUSTED *ALL* TO *HELL*. THIS ISN'T GOING TO HEAL RIGHT *AT ALL*, RICK... NOT EVEN *CLOSE*.

I *DON'T* THINK YOU'LL EVEN BE ABLE TO *USE* IT.

I'LL WORRY ABOUT THAT *LATER*--YOU JUST *CLEAN* IT. I DON'T WANT IT TO GET *INFECTED* ON *TOP* OF EVERYTHING ELSE.

I DON'T REGRET A THING.

YOU'RE OFF THE HOOK. IT *WASN'T* YOU.

THAT IT? THAT *ALL* YOU GONNA SAY?

THAT'S IT. YOU GOING TO START SOME *TROUBLE?*

YOU STILL GOT ALL THE *GUNS?*

YEAH. EVERY LAST *ONE* OF THEM.

THOUGH AFTER WHAT *WE'VE* JUST BEEN THROUGH THE LAST THING WE WANT TO DO IS *USE* THEM.

THAT SO? GOOD NEWS, I GUESS.

WHO *WAS* IT? DID IT I MEAN. *ALLEN?* THAT WAS HIS NAME *RIGHT?* HE SURE *LOOKED* CRAZY ENOUGH.

ONE OF *YOURS.* THOMAS-- THE "TAX EVADER."

HMM. I DIDN'T KNOW *WHAT* HE WAS IN FOR, BUT I *KNEW* IT WASN'T *TAX EVASION.* NEVER DID TRUST HIM.

DON'T TRUST *A LOT* OF PEOPLE NOW.

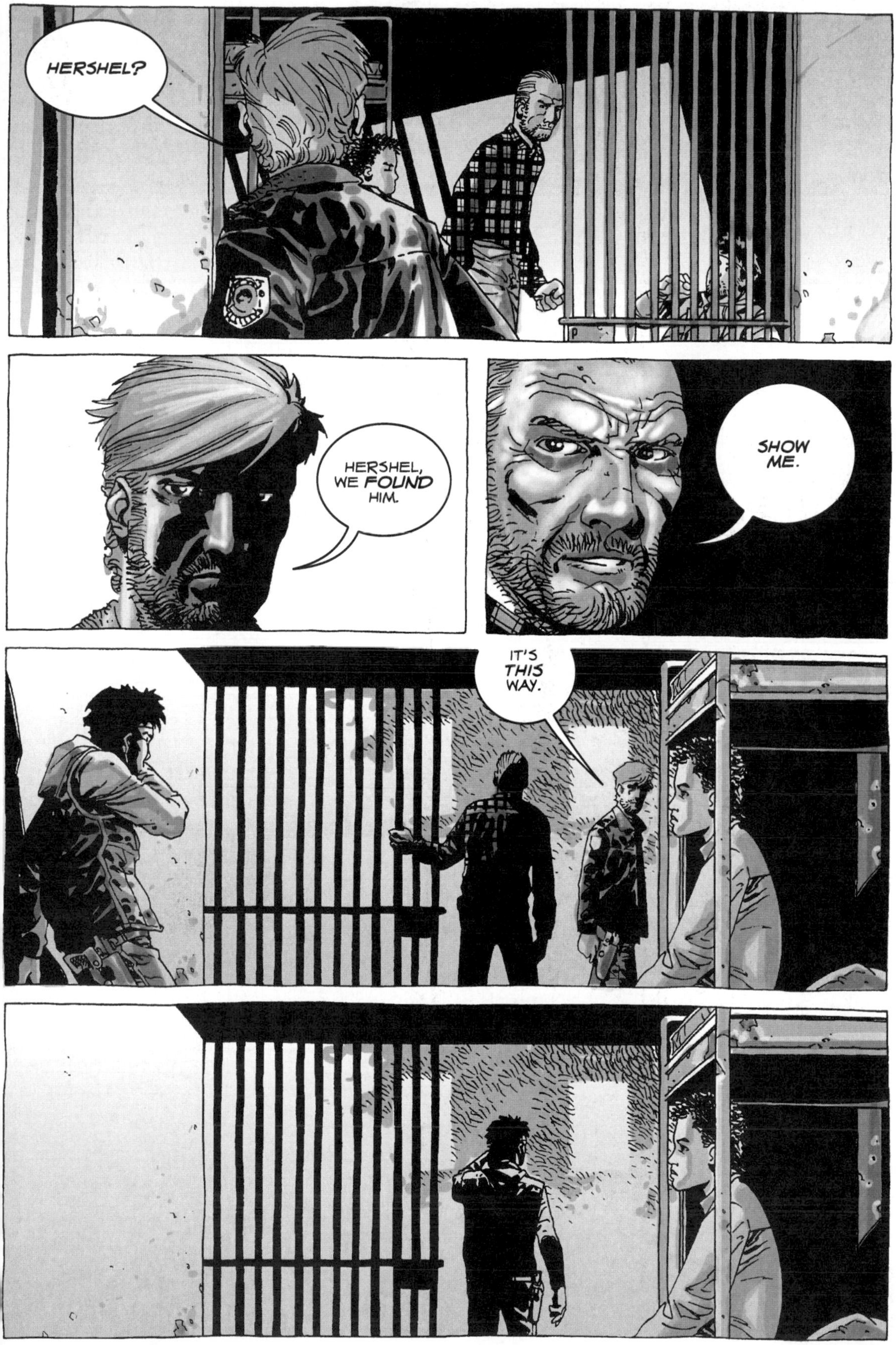
HERSHEL?
HERSHEL, WE FOUND HIM.
SHOW ME.
IT'S THIS WAY.

GUYS--WHERE THE *FUCK* IS HE? WHAT DID YOU *DO* WITH HIM?

PUT THE *WASTE* WITH THE *WASTE*-- THOUGHT IT MIGHT MAKE HIS WAIT AS UNPLEASANT AS IT *SHOULD* BE.

JUST PUTTING HIM *IN* THERE WAS KILLING ME.

IF YOU DIDN'T BREAK HIS *NOSE* TOO BAD--HE'S *NOT* ENJOYING HIMSELF.

THERE'S NO *VENTILATION* IN THERE! HE'LL *SUFFOCATE* BEFORE WE CAN *HANG* HIM. THAT'S TOO *GOOD* FOR HIM.

GET HIM *OUT* OF THERE.

DIDN'T THINK OF *THAT.* I JUST LIKED THE IDEA OF HIM WALLOWING IN HIS OWN *SHIT.*

TAKE HIM AND LOCK HIM IN A *CELL* WHILE WE GATHER UP MATERIALS. WE'LL THROW HIM OUT OF A *GUARD TOWER* WITH A *ROPE* AROUND HIS NECK. THAT'LL TAKE CARE OF HIM.

I WILL LET THE *LORD* BE YOUR *JUDGE.*

I WANT YOU TO *KNOW* THAT I *FORGIVE* YOU.

HERSHEL-- WE'RE *STILL* GOING TO *HANG* HIM.

I KNOW.

I WANT TO *WATCH.*

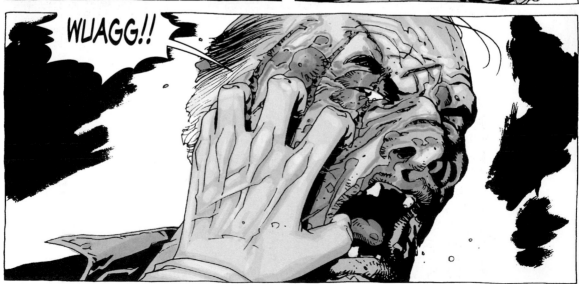

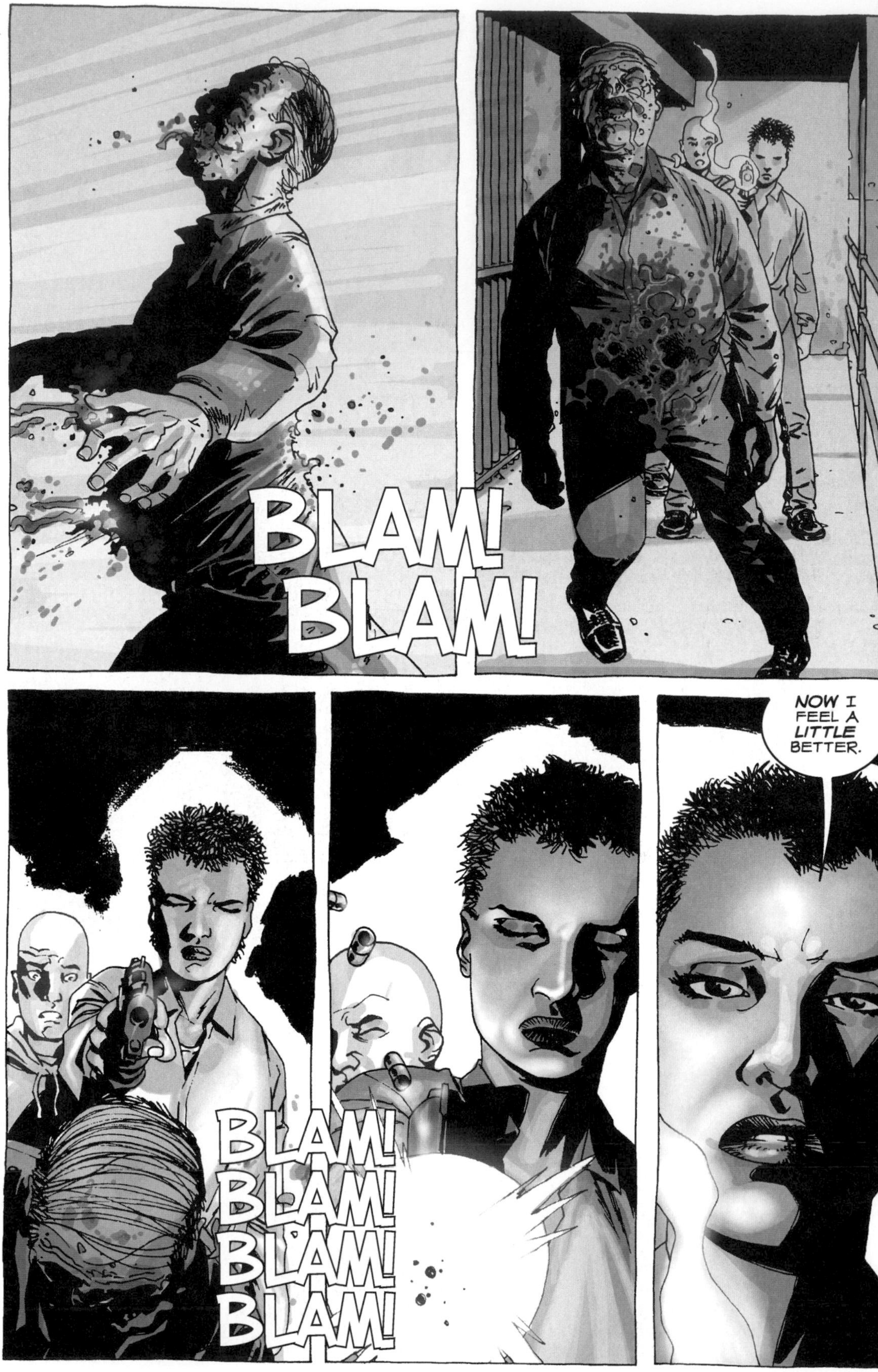
BLAM! BLAM!
BLAM! BLAM! BLAM! BLAM!
NOW I FEEL A LITTLE BETTER.

JESUS CHRIST!

BE READY TO CLOSE THAT GATE IN A *HURRY* ONCE WE GET BACK *INSIDE.*

YOU GUYS *READY?*

IF I WASN'T--I'D DO IT *ANYWAY* SO WE COULD GET BACK *INSIDE.*

LET'S-- *UNG*-- DO IT.

THIS--*THIS* I *DON'T* NEED TO SEE.

IT **OVER?** IS IT **SAFE** TO BRING THEM **OUT?**

YEAH-- JUST DON'T LET THEM GET IN **VIEWING** DISTANCE OF THE FRONT PARIMETER OF THE GROUNDS.

OF **COURSE.**

SO--HE'S JUST OUT THERE... **WATCHING?**

IT WAS **HIS IDEA.** I GUESS HE'S GETTING SOME KIND OF **CLOSURE** OUT OF IT. I PREFER NOT TO **THINK** ABOUT IT.

WHERE **IS** PATRICIA? HAVE YOU **SEEN** HER SINCE ALL THE--

NO. WHAT ARE YOU GOING TO **DO** WITH HER?

WHAT **CAN I DO?** IT'S NOT LIKE WE CAN **BEAT** HER OR JUST LOCK HER UP-- WE'RE NOT **ANIMALS.** I'M GOING TO **TALK** WITH HER, I GUESS.

AIN'T **NO NEED** FOR THAT. SHE'S WITH **US.**

MORE GREAT TITLES FROM
ROBERT KIRKMAN & IMAGE

ROBERT KIRKMAN TONY MOORE
THE WALKING DEAD
VOLUME 1
DAYS GONE BYE

THE WALKING DEAD, VOL. 1:
DAYS GONE BYE
ISBN# 1-58240-358-9
TRADE PAPERBACK
$9.95

ROBERT KIRKMAN CHARLIE ADLARD CLIFF RATHBURN
THE WALKING DEAD
VOLUME 2
MILES BEHIND US

THE WALKING DEAD, VOL. 2:
DAYS GONE BYE
ISBN# 1-58240-413-5
TRADE PAPERBACK
$12.95

KIRKMAN • WALKER • CRABTREE
INVINCIBLE
CRISIS AVERTED
FAMILY MATTERS

INVINCIBLE, VOL. 1:
FAMILY MATTERS
ISBN# 1-58240-320-1
TRADE PAPERBACK
$12.95

KIRKMAN • WALKER • OTTLEY • CRABTREE
INVINCIBLE
EIGHT IS ENOUGH
Introduction by Erik Larsen

INVINCIBLE, VOL. 2:
EIGHT IS ENOUGH
ISBN# 1-58240-347-3
TRADE PAPERBACK
$12.95

KIRKMAN • OTTLEY • CRABTREE
INVINCIBLE
PERFECT STRANGERS
Introduction by Tom Brevoort

INVINCIBLE, VOL. 3:
PERFECT STRANGERS
ISBN# 1-58240-391-0
TRADE PAPERBACK
$12.95

KIRKMAN • OTTLEY • CRABTREE
INVINCIBLE
HEAD OF THE CLASS
Introduction by Mark Waid

INVINCIBLE, VOL. 4:
HEAD OF THE CLASS
ISBN# 1-58240-440-2
TRADE PAPERBACK
$12.95

BRIT
COLD DEATH
ROBERT KIRKMAN & TONY MOORE

BRIT: COLD DEATH
ISBN# 1-58240-386-4
PRESTIGE FORMAT
$4.95

BRIT
RED WHITE BLACK & BLUE
ROBERT KIRKMAN
CLIFF RATHBURN

BRIT: RED WHITE BLACK & BLUE
ISBN# 1-58240-378-3
PRESTIGE FORMAT
$4.95

TECH JACKET

TECH JACKET, VOL. 1:
LOST AND FOUND
ISBN# 1-58240-314-7
TRADE PAPERBACK
$12.95

For The Comic Shop Near You Carrying Comics And Collections From Image Comics,
Please Call Toll Free 1-888-Comic Book.

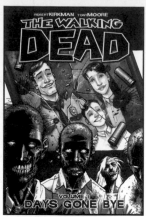

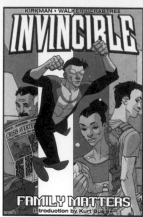